Machiavelli
The Prince

Translated by C. E. Detmold

Introduction by Lucille Margaret Kekewich

WORDSWORTH CLASSICS
OF WORLD LITERATURE

In loving memory of
MICHAEL TRAYLER
the founder of Wordsworth Editions

7

Readers who are interested in other titles from
Wordsworth Editions are invited to visit our website at
www.wordsworth-editions.com

For our latest list and a full mail-order service, contact
Bibliophile Books, 5 Thomas Road, London E14 7BN
TEL: +44 (0)20 7515 9222 FAX: +44 (0)20 7538 4115
E-MAIL: orders@bibliophilebooks.com

This edition published 1997 by Wordsworth Editions Limited
8B East Street, Ware, Hertfordshire SG12 9HJ

ISBN 978-1-85326-775-8

Typeset in Great Britain by Antony Gray
Printed and bound by Clays Ltd, St Ives plc

WORDSWORTH CLASSICS
OF WORLD LITERATURE

General Editor: Tom Griffith

THE PRINCE

CONTENTS

APPENDICES

INTRODUCTION

The making of a theorist: negotium

Between 1494 and 1498 much of the population of Florence had been gripped by a kind of religious revivalism, inspired to a great extent by the apparent fulfilment of a prophecy made by Fra Girolamo Savonarola. He had predicted that Italy would be invaded by the armies of the French king as a punishment for its sins. Sure enough in 1494 Charles VIII had invaded and Piero de' Medici, the unofficial head of the Florentine state, fled, leaving Florence to God and the patricians. Despite the Christian fervour felt by many people, it did not prove to be a sound basis for the restoration of republican rule. Some former Medici supporters, and others who disliked Savonarola's style of moral leadership, succeeded in undermining his credibility as a holy man and eventually managed to utilise his condemnation by the Papacy to have him burned (Appendix A: Guicciardini, *History of Florence*, 16). It was just after these traumatic events that Niccolò Machiavelli achieved the position of second chancellor (secretary) to the republic. He started a career of *negotium*, or public service, which provided the raw material for his later life as a writer, when another violent political change forced him out of the government into *otium*, or a leisurely existence.

Machiavelli entered the inner circles of government influenced by two very different political experiences: the domination of one great family and the brief theocracy of Savonarola. He had been born in 1467, the year when Lorenzo and Giuliano de' Medici succeeded their father as the leading citizens of Florence. The city and its territories remained in theory a republic ruled by a series of councils and elected officials. In practice, since the middle years of the fifteenth century, all organs of government had been dominated by the powerful and wealthy family of the Medici and its supporters. After his brother Giuliano's assassination, Lorenzo (the Magnificent) presided over a state which achieved enormous prestige and influence through the work of its scholars and artists, but which enjoyed very limited political power. Fortunately for the integrity of Florence, none of the other principal states of Italy – Milan, Venice, Naples and the Papal States – had sufficient force at their disposal to pose a serious threat. The death of Lorenzo de' Medici in 1492, when Machiavelli was in his twenties, marked the beginning of a turbulent period in Italian politics.

The new pope, Alexander VI, was anxious to establish his children, especially Cesare Borgia, in rich principalities. The corruption and profligacy of the Papacy was a major theme in the sermons of Savonarola, and set it on a collision course with Florence. The French king's presence meant that any state which could win his support would enjoy a great advantage over its rivals, unless they could attract yet more foreign aid from either the emperor or the King of Spain. So there were many lessons which an observant and ambitious young man could learn from the brutal de-stabilisation of Italy which occurred in the 1490s. The strongest of his political instincts seems to have been to favour the republican form of government. By this Machiavelli and his contemporaries did not mean a democracy on the twentieth century French or American model, but a state controlled by its citizens. Citizenship was a privilege confined to native-born males who owned sufficient property to give them a right to a voice. A relatively small proportion of the population of Florence would have qualified as citizens in the fifteenth century, and even after the demise of the Medici, a limited number of families held most of the power. Machiavelli's preference for a republic was, however, modified by an appreciation of the difficulties and dangers faced by the Italian states. For this reason he did not discount the possibility of princely rule when circumstances required it. The Medici regime had after all safeguarded the independence of Florence. What he disliked above all was a government which was motivated by ideology: Savonarola's intransigence had increased the danger of losing the benefits gained from the flight of the Medici. It was fine to proclaim the supremacy of religion and morality, but it was fatal to sacrifice the interests of the state in their defence.

Machiavelli's republicanism cannot solely be explained by his Florentine birth: a humanist education would have instilled the same values. Most of what is known of his early life comes from the diary of his father: Bernardo Machiavelli was a lawyer, a landowner on a modest scale, and a humanist. He was the partner of Bartolomeo Scala in a dialogue about the law which survives in the Archives at Siena. Scala was first chancellor to the republic until his death in 1497, and it may have been through his good offices that Niccolò Machiavelli was given a post. His education had prepared him for the high standards expected of a Florentine civil servant, for sixteen years earlier his father had put him to school with a highly respected humanist, Paolo Ronciglione.

A principal part of the motor which drove the Italian Renaissance in the fifteenth and sixteenth centuries was the enormous respect felt by scholars, artists and politicians for Roman antiquity. It was generally accepted that Rome had been at her greatest whilst she adhered to her republican institutions, putting strong armies in the field with which she united the Italian peninsula under her rule and started to build up an empire. Her senate and public servants were patriotic and incorruptible, her women virtuous and her children obedient. Her decline and ultimate fall was caused by the emperors, who perverted her institutions for their own selfish purposes. It followed that a regeneration of Italian society and political life could best be achieved by a return to the values held under the Roman republic. The work of Hans Baron (especially *The Crisis of the Early Italian Renaissance*) has demonstrated that this nostalgia for the Roman past was heightened during the early Renaissance by writers and jurists who saw in the free city republics of Italy the revival of what was best in antiquity.

The destruction of Savonarola did not also entail the dismemberment of the Florentine republic. Its institutions had survived throughout the period of Medici rule and had been enhanced in 1494, when Piero fled, by the introduction of a Great Council, 'the soul of the city'. (Felix Gilbert, 9) Its functions were to vote, but not to discuss, taxes and to choose the members of a series of committees, which carried out the executive functions of government. As second chancellor Machiavelli worked most closely with the Ten of War: despite their alarming title they were mainly concerned with foreign relations and in avoiding involvement in wars. Yet the republic was already embroiled in one destructive internal conflict: its subject city of Pisa, an important port and trading outlet, had revolted immediately after the Medici left, and the war to subdue it dragged on for ten years. Other problems which beset the Ten and their chancellor were the presence of the French in Italy and of Cesare Borgia, supported by the pope his father, on their borders. The Florentines were traditionally the allies of the French, but the king expected unswerving loyalty and large sums of money as the price of his not very effective support.

Throughout his fourteen years as chancellor Machiavelli was regularly sent on missions both to the allies of Florence and to her potential enemies. Whilst the republic was fortunate enough not to be one of the many Italian states to which the great foreign powers could legitimately make a claim, most of them instinctively distrusted a people who had ejected their ruler. Although the hapless Piero de' Medici was soon killed in battle he had plenty of relations who were pressing for the restoration of their house, and one of them was an influential cardinal. Machiavelli learnt much from his diplomatic missions: his views can be recovered both from the many reports he sent back to his masters and from his later writings. Four visits to Louis XII of France taught him how insignificant the Italian states were in power and wealth in comparison with the greater European powers. He received very little support from his own government which, because of the dispersed nature of its authority, seemed weak and vacillating besides a monarchy where decisions could be taken swiftly and necessary resources provided rapidly (Quentin Skinner, *Machiavelli*, chapter 1).

Machiavelli's encounters with Cesare Borgia, duke of Valentino, are famously recorded in *The Prince*. His initial meetings impressed him greatly: here was a man of action unburdened by ideological or moral baggage which could impede his rise to power in central Italy. But Cesare's fortune lasted only as long as his father's life: his ruthless daring was no match for the new pope, Julius II, who was just as ruthless and a great deal more powerful. By the time of Cesare's sudden death a few years later, fighting as a mercenary for the king of Navarre, Machiavelli had realised how badly the duke had miscalculated, but this did not prevent him from using him as a model in his later writings.

Machiavelli did not get the full measure of Julius II on his visit to Rome in 1503, when he reported the process of his election. Three years later, when he followed the formidable pontiff around central Italy, he had formed a better idea of his capacities and ambition. Retrospectively he saw that Julius had further destabilised the balance of power in Italy, already undermined by French incursions, and created the conditions which allowed the emperor and Spain to exploit it for their own ends. In 1507 Machiavelli had an opportunity to study German political institutions at close quarters as he and Francesco Vettori, who was to become his lifelong friend, were sent to discover the intentions of the Emperor Maximilian towards Italy. They achieved very little for, as Sydney Anglo said, Maximilian's ' . . . schemes were . . . shrouded in the inpenetrable secrecy of those who haven't the faintest idea of what they are doing' (p. 23). Instructions from the Florentine government were unsatisfactory and often – conveyed in such unpromising containers as messengers' boots and loaves of bread – illegible. Machiavelli formed a low opinion of Maximilian. He invariably preferred men of action to procrastinators. He did, however, admire the way in which the German city states functioned within the empire, seeing them as retaining some of the excellence of the ancient Roman republic (Appendix B, i, *Discourses* 1, 55).

Increasingly the energies of Machiavelli and his masters had to be concentrated on the dangerous situation on their own borders. The alliance of Julius II and France, which had allowed them to make depredations on the Italian states unchecked, broke down and changed to mutual hostility. This did not suit Florence, since both powers expected her support. After unsuccessful attempts to please both sides the republic adhered to her traditional friendship with France, but there were no French armies available to protect her, and it was an easy matter for the Pope to restore the Medici. The soldiers of his ally, the king of Spain, invaded Florentine territory in 1512 and besieged the town of Prato. The local militia, who were meant to defend it, had been organised by Machiavelli a few years earlier in an attempt to dispense with mercenary armies. They failed miserably and the town fell. The terms for peace included the return of the Medici led by Giuliano, a son of Lorenzo the Magnificent. He already enjoyed the support of a faction amongst the patricians of the city, and immediately set about dismantling republican institutions, especially the Great Council. He even had the hall where it had met demolished. There was no bloodbath, but some leading members of the previous regime went into exile, and Machiavelli was dismissed from office. He suffered an even greater misfortune in the following year when he was falsely accused of participating in a futile little plot against the Medici. He was imprisoned and tortured but maintained his innocence. After a swift release he retired to his farm at San Casciano, about seven miles from Florence. He spent most of the rest of his life there, always hoping that he would be re-employed by the state and nearly always being disappointed.

The work of retirement: otium

(I) THE PRINCE

In the early years of his enforced retirement Machiavelli filled his time by supervising work on his land, drinking and playing cards in the local tavern, reading and writing (Appendix C, letter to Franceso Vettori). He had, of course, been writing for many years and his first treatise, The Prince, most closely resembles the numerous letters and reports which he had sent back to the Florentine government during his career as second chancellor. It was dedicated in 1513 to the newly restored Giuliano de' Medici, offering him 'knowledge of the actions of great men, which I have acquired by long experience of modern affairs and a continued study of ancient history' in the hope that 'you attain that greatness which fortune and your great qualities promise' (Dedication, 3-4). The Dedication ended with an ill-disguised plea to be restored to favour. On Giuliano's death a few years later, Machiavelli re-dedicated the treatise to his nephew and successor Lorenzo.

Machiavelli's duplicity in explaining how a prince might gain and keep supreme power in a state, and do so by ruthless and amoral means, has frequently been remarked upon. This work, above all others, gave him the reputation for advocating the unprincipled pursuit of power unrestrained by conventional religious or ethical standards. The fact that he wrote it immediately after the fall of the republic which he had served with such enthusiasm, exacerbated his crime and seemed to reflect the recommendations he made in the treatise. There are three particular features of *The Prince* which have been singled out for comment by later writers and which seem to distinguish it from the considerable body of such works produced by Machiavelli's predecessors and contemporaries (See Q. Skinner, *Foundations of Modern Political Thought* 1, 113-38). He replaced the traditional requirement that a successful ruler was one who embodied Christian virtues such as honesty and clemency, with the view that, above all, he should have sufficient force at his disposal to establish his undisputed control. A ruler should, as far as possible, observe conventional standards of morality, but provided he gave the *appearance* of doing so, he could act in a dishonest and ruthless fashion when it suited his interests. Machiavelli concluded his treatise with an appeal to the Medici to take the lead amongst the rulers of Italy in expelling the barbarians (the various non-Italian invaders), and to restore harmony and unity of purpose. A more detailed examination of the work will show just how original and outrageous he was being in making these suggestions.

The Prince starts conventionally enough by discussing the different kinds of governments to be found in states: a form of analysis which originated with Greek writers on politics, notably Aristotle. Instead of providing a conventional description of three types of state – monarchies, aristocracies and democracies (and their perversions: tyrannies, oligarchies and anarchy) – Machiavelli confines himself to principates and republics, probably because these approximated more closely to what was to be found in Italy. Many of the states, including Florence, contained both princely and republican elements in their organisation. He offers no judgement about which is the better form of government, simply remarking that he will concentrate on the former as he has discussed republics at length elsewhere (in the *Discourses*, see below). He devotes most of his attention to new princes because a ruler from a long-established dynasty 'has less cause and less necessity for irritating his subjects, whence it is reasonable that he should be more beloved. And unless extraordinary vices should cause him to be hated, he will naturally have the affection of his people'. (chapter 2, 6)

Machiavelli spends most of the first part of his treatise (chapters 3 – 11) in discussing how new princes can secure their position, and the dangers that have to be avoided. He cites many examples from ancient and contemporary history to confirm his arguments. The failure of Louis XII of France to secure a permanent principality in Italy is attributed, amongst other things, to his introduction of Spanish power into the peninsula, undermining his vulnerable allies amongst the city states, and to the fact that he neither remained in the country nor established colonies directly ruled by France. Machiavelli is less sure of himself when dealing with the subjection of states which have been accustomed to 'liberty and the government of their own laws'. The recent experience of the Pisan revolt leads him to conclude that 'the surest way of holding them is either to destroy them, or for the conqueror to go and live there' (chapter 5, 19). States acquired by a prince courageously leading his own troops to conquest may initially present a challenge but, once they are subdued by force, they will settle down under his rule. On the other hand, those acquired with the help of others or by Fortune may prove difficult to hold. Machiavelli quotes at length from the career of Cesare Borgia to exemplify his points, suggesting that the duke did everything to secure his position as a conqueror of papal territories; but the misfortune of the death of his father, the Pope, which coincided with his own debilitating illness, led to his downfall. This was compounded by his misjudgement in allowing Julius II to be elected pope: 'whosoever thinks that amongst great personages recent benefits will cause old injuries to be forgotten, deceives himself greatly.' (chapter 7, 31)

In describing examples, ancient and modern, of princes who have gained their position by cruelty and deceit, Machiavelli condemns their crimes whilst expressing some admiration for their success. His conclusion is that if harsh measures are necessary to secure a state, it is better to take them all at once, and then rule justly to restore the confidence of one's subjects. Conversely, in the case of princes chosen by their own people or nobility, their main concern in order to retain power must be to rule according to the wishes or interests of their subjects. The other requirement for security is to have sufficient money to be able to put a strong army in the field and to fortify the main cities against attack. As far as ecclesiastical states are concerned, Machiavelli's main advice is 'Don't mess with the Church!' He gives a brief review of how recent able and determined popes have built up their temporal power, and concludes with a cringing tribute to the new pope Leo X (the brother of Giuliano de' Medici): 'it is to be hoped that, if his predecessors have made the Church great by means of arms, he will make her greater and more venerable by his goodness and his infinite other virtues.' (chapter 11, 46)

Machiavelli summarises his advice about how princes should acquire and keep control of their states by stressing the importance of good military skills They should take personal control of the army, exercise and discipline it well even in peacetime, and study the art of war scientifically. Hunting expeditions are also recommended as they toughen their bodies and enable them to study different kinds of terrain (necessary for planning strategy). Machiavelli devotes two chapters to his obsessive dislike of mercenary and auxiliary troops: he defines the latter as soldiers lent to a prince by a foreign power. Both kinds will put their own interests before those of their employer (the uselessness of French troops in the war against Pisa is cited), and if they can be persuaded to engage in battle, they will probably be defeated. Matters will be even worse in the unlikely event of a victory, as they can become powerful enough to dislodge the prince. If a prince wishes to resist the reverses of Fortune, the best policy is to employ armies drawn from within the state. Machiavelli wrote this a matter of months after the rout of the militia he had raised for the defence of Prato.

The next section of the treatise can be interpreted as a kind of satire on conventional mirrors for princes: books which advocate the possession of the four cardinal virtues – justice, prudence, temperance and fortitude – plus some particularly regal qualities such as liberality and clemency. The genre had been developed in the late middle ages, and numerous treatises by prominent scholars such as Thomas Aquinas and Vincent of Beauvais had been addressed to rulers in Italy, France and England. They shared the basic premise that successful princes ruled according to high standards of Christian morality. So Machiavelli was writing within a well-known tradition which was immediately recognisable to his readers, and there is every indication that he expected his ideas to be taken seriously. His justification for subverting the accepted rules of princely behaviour was that 'a man who, in all respects, will carry out only his professions of good, will be apt to be ruined amongst so many who are evil.' (chapter 15, 59)

A prince should certainly try to be good and should shun vices which might make him so unpopular that he would be overthrown, but it is better to practise vices which will preserve his position than virtues which will destroy it. It is, for example, dangerous to be too generous since it can lead the prince into poverty. The taxation he will be obliged to levy to restore his prosperity will make him more unpopular than if he has been parsimonious from the beginning. Turning traditional values on their heads again, Machiavelli praises Hannibal for his notorious cruelty, as it enabled him to control his immense army. Scipio's renowned clemency, on the other hand, could have led the state to ruin if it had not been favourably manipulated by the Roman senate.

Chapter 18, 'In What Manner Princes Should Keep Their Faith', has probably been both the most reviled and the most emulated passage in all Machiavelli's works. Later writers were to use his thinking, often unattributed, to develop the justification of 'reasons of state' for taking unprincipled action, for a prince was 'often obliged, for the sake of maintaining his state, to act contrary to humanity, charity and religion'. (68)

In his dealings, a wise prince should combine the strength of the lion with the cunning of the fox. Two excellent modern examples of the successful exercise of power and duplicity were Pope Alexander VI and King Ferdinand of Aragon. What made them so effective was that they both paid lip service with great conviction to Christian standards of morality. It is essential for a prince to avoid unpopularity, for if a substantial proportion of his subjects hate him, conspiracies are likely to succeed. In Chapter 19, Machiavelli's terse style gets bogged down in numerous examples drawn from the disastrous careers of later Roman emperors. The very wealth of detail prevents clear conclusions from being drawn from his narrative; and some of the details seem to contradict points made elsewhere.

Machiavelli resumes his concise style in reviewing the practical measures that princes should take to safeguard their positions. There is no firm rule about arming subjects or building fortresses but, always depending on particular circumstances, it is better to trust citizens with weapons, and avoid building defences against them, as the greatest assurance of security is to be popular. Successful wars both channel the energies of subjects away from internal dissent and enhance a prince's reputation. This maxim is supported by a very acute analysis of how Ferdinand of Aragon rose from obscurity, initially by the conquest of Granada and then by the Italian wars, 'to become the first sovereign of Christendom'. (chapter 21, 84) It is equally important to keep a fine court, encourage artists and traders, 'at suitable periods amuse his people with festivities and spectacles', 'occasionally be present at their [guild] assemblies, and . . . set an example of affability and magnificence'. (chapter 21, 87) The choice of ministers and advisers also reflects the quality of the prince. The best will put his interests before their own. He should discourage unsolicited advice (a disconcerting sentiment considering the dedication of the treatise), but when it is required should use his own discrimination in accepting or rejecting it.

The last three chapters of *The Prince* address what Machiavelli believes to be the greatest evil in the Italy of his day: the domination of foreign powers. Princes such as the King of Naples and the Duke of Milan had lost their states through neglect of the kind of principles which had been formulated in the treatise. In a vivid passage he compares the operation of fortune 'to a swollen river, which in its fury overflows the plains, tears up the trees and buildings, and sweeps the earth from one place and deposits it in another. Everyone flies before the flood, and yields to its fury, unable to resist it . . . It is the same with fortune, who displays her power where there is no organised valour to resist her'. (chapter 25, 94). Apart from making prudent preparations to avoid disasters, it is best to act audaciously. As a woman fortune favours the young and the energetic, and is more likely to be controlled by them. Finally Machiavelli appeals to the Medici to take the lead in expelling the foreign armies from Italy. In this chapter he abandons the measured, cynical tones of a political commentator and writes with the messianic fervour that he must have encountered as a young man living in the Florence of Savonarola. He also sets aside the realism which has informed his earlier advice. The Medici were neither willing nor able to play the part Machiavelli had assigned to them, and the proposal was unlikely to improve the prospects of the disgraced politician.

Throughout *The Prince* there is a constant tension between 'fortune' and 'virtue' – concepts which have greatly preoccupied commentators on Machiavelli. As a good humanist he gives Fortune all the attributes of the classical goddess, but he can scarcely have believed in the objective existence of such a supernatural force. It is clear from the context in which the references occur that he uses 'fortune' as a metaphor for political upheavals, especially violent and unexpected ones. Princes should do their best to anticipate such dangers, but can never be entirely certain of success. The illness of Cesare Borgia at a crisis in his career was an example of this phenomenon. The best means a prince can use to offset the power of 'fortune', or the unexpected, in his affairs was to exercise 'virtue' (depending on the context Detmold, our translator, sometimes calls it 'valour'). The Italian word for this quality is 'virtù', and by it Machiavelli certainly does not mean traditional Christian virtues such as charity, humility and compassion: rather he sees it as deriving from the Latin 'virtus', power and energy. It is, however, a moral as well as a physical force, operating on behalf of the state, as well as its ruler, for the common good. The ambiguity of 'virtue' as it is used by Machiavelli, and the difficulty of providing an exact translation, contributed to the hostility with which his treatise was received. In any case, how could someone be taken seriously who, at about the same time, had written a long book in praise of republican government?

(II) OTHER MAJOR WORKS

The Prince did not achieve any preferment for Machiavelli, and he progressively put his energies into his work as a writer. A stimulus came from a circle of humanists who met regularly for discussions in the Oricellari Gardens on the outskirts of Florence. The reference in Chapter 2 (see p. xiii) implies that he had already drafted his *Discourses* on Livy by the time he had finished *The*

Prince, but he probably refined his ideas about the main theme of the former, what determined the success or failure of republics, by further reading and discussion up to their completion in 1518/19. Commentators who start with the proposition that the *Discourses* represent a different stage in Machiavelli's thinking from that found in *The Prince* encounter all manner of anomalies. Almost all the major arguments found in *The Prince* also occur in the *Discourses*. He makes it clear by his reference to them in the former work that he regards both treatises as forming part of the same piece of political analysis.

The *Discourses* were dedicated to Cosimo Rucellai, the owner of the Oricellari Gardens, and another member of the circle which met there, Zanobi Buondelmonte. They had evidently been discussing political systems and had asked Machiavelli to write something which reflected his long practical experience of the subject. Just as *The Prince* investigates the factors which contribute to the success or failure of a princely regime, the *Discourses* take Livy's *History* of Rome as a starting point for a dissection of its republican phase and in particular an identification of the features which first ensured its great success and subsequently its decline. Whilst stressing that its citizens, as well as the leading magistrates, should possess 'virtue', its operation within a political context was expected to achieve the same kinds of goals as those he had set in *The Prince*: victory over enemies, strong citizen armies, sound institutions and a religion which reinforced the power of the state (Appendix B, ii, *Discourses* II. 2). There would be times, however, when authority would have to be given to one wise man and, as in *The Prince*, he would be justified in taking unprincipled actions for the good of the state (Appendix B, iii, *Discourses* I.9).

Quentin Skinner has demonstrated that in making Livy his starting point, and in drawing on other classical writers such as Sallust, as well as Italians who praised the ideals of civic humanism, Machiavelli was writing within a well-known tradition which supported republican forms of government ('Machiavelli's *Discorsi* and the pre-humanist origins of republican ideas', *Machiavelli and Republicanism*, 121–41). Circumstances dictate whether a particular country was best constituted as a princely or republican state: this opinion is entirely consistent with Machiavelli's innovatory approach to political ideas. For him decisions should always be taken to promote the best possible result rather than to accord with some abstract system of morality or belief.

The discussion group which met in the Oricellari Gardens seems to have been the inspiration for Machiavelli's next major work, *The Art of War*, which he wrote in 1520. It was published in the following year and enjoyed a certain popularity for a while, but as Sydney Anglo remarked:

'Far from being the first modern treatise on warfare, it would be more properly regarded as perhaps the greatest – though certainly not the last – medieval compilation.' (157) Machiavelli was heavily reliant on late classical authorities such as Vegetius and Frontinus, although he also retains the practice of illustrating his argument from modern examples. The trouble was that his dependence on the wisdom of antiquity discouraged him from engaging with the profound changes which had taken place over the last century. For example, he had a low opinion of the usefulness of artillery. The book was mainly a vehicle for reiterating his faith in the efficacy of a militia as opposed to mercenary or auxiliary troops, and only information which supported this opinion was employed (Appendix D, *Art of War*, Book 1).

By the mid-1520s the disposition of the Medici rulers of Florence had changed for the better as far as Machiavelli was concerned. Pope Leo X had been replaced by his gentler cousin, Clement VII. Lay members of the family were either minors or nonentities, and at last the old politician started to get some employment. He acted as an emissary on several occasions, and was commissioned to write a *History of Florence*: he presented the completed work to Clement in 1525. Commentators have frequently expostulated against the contradictions inherent in his last great book. Whilst retaining his faith that the republican form of government was the best for a city state such as Florence, he had to pay due deference to the Medici. Judged by modern standards, Machiavelli is not a satisfactory historian: he provides a quick jog through Florentine history up to the fourteenth century, and then dwells on the episodes which interest him most, or which are least likely to cause embarrassment to his patron. The last book finishes in 1492 with the death of Lorenzo the Magnificent: the author is understandably reluctant to deal with the anti-Medicean regime in which he had played a prominent part (Appendix E, *History*, Book 8, 36).

In 1526 Machiavelli wrote an account of the fortifications of Florence, which he had recently inspected on behalf of the state with a military expert, Pietro Navarro. He at last recovered the position of importance which he had lost back in 1512. He was made Secretary to the Procurators of the Walls. This interest in the city's defences, however, was ominous: Clement VII feared that he would be attacked by the Imperial army. A year later Rome was sacked and his hegemony in Florence was destroyed. Ironically the young men who took over did not remember Machiavelli's services to the previous republic and saw him as a collaborator with the Medici. He lost his post, fell ill, and died in June 1527. He just missed the siege of Florence which eventually resulted in the restoration (this time for good) of the Medici. One of the reasons why the republicans were able to hold out for so long was probably the quality of the improvements in the fortifications which Machiavelli had initiated.

Machiavelli and posterity: fama

Fame (fama) or good reputation was a major aspiration for the writers and artists of the Renaissance, so how has Machiavelli's credit stood in the four and a half centuries since his death? It is hard to be neutral about him. Even in the late twentieth century when much of what he wrote has become the common currency of *realpolitik*, his ideas retain the capacity to shock and annoy. Despite the admiration of the circle in the Oricellari Gardens, his views were called in question even during his lifetime and soon after his death.

Francesco Guicciardini, a writer and diplomat, knew Machiavelli and outlived him long enough to produce several histories and works on contemporary politics, as well as a commentary on the *Discourses* (Appendix F, *Commentary*, chapter 3). Unlike Machiavelli, most of his public service was done for the Medici, and as an aristocratic man of means he could sometimes be expected to disagree with Machiavelli's views. Guicciardini expressed moderate enthusiasm for a republican form of government for Florence. It could be viable, but only if it contained elements of monarchy (a head of state appointed for life) and aristocracy (a senate). Here we have a version of the old mixed constitution of Aristotle which had been so influential on medieval scholars. In his commentary on the *Discourses* (1530) he showed 'his distrust of Machiavelli's tendency to theorise and to draw what he would consider to be sweeping conclusions from inadequate evidence'. (Nicolai Rubenstein, Introduction, *Maxims*, 19)

He also queried the wisdom of prescribing policies for rulers which went against their natural inclinations: 'Princes will often do what they please or what they know, and not what they should'. (Guicciardini, *Ibid.* 73)

And it was a mistake to assume that the ancient Roman republic was invariably a suitable model on which to base policies in sixteenth century Italy. Cecil Grayson neatly characterises the essential difference between Machiavelli and Guicciardini 'as a contrast between a broad idealistic vision of man's capabilities, characteristic of fifteenth century humanism, and a limited view of his capacities in a world of haphazard events' (Introduction, *Selected Writings*, ed. C. Grayson, xv).

If Machiavelli's fellow-countryman, Guicciardini, expressed reservations about his theories for practical reasons, the reactions of other European writers in the sixteenth and following centuries were primarily based on moral outrage. The Wars of Religion in France initiated a polemical and ideological battle of great ferocity. All the factions employed arguments drawn from Machiavelli's works to justify their pragmatic reaction to circumstances, but they also roundly condemned him for his lack of principle. His ideas were initially received with respect in England, but by the second half of the century they came to be identified with foreign, catholic duplicity. Insults abounded, such as: 'A Scurvie Schollar of Machiavellus Lair' (F. Raab, *English Face of Machiavelli*, 58). In the next century, during the Civil War and Interregnum, his republicanism restored him to favour with anti-monarchists such as James Harrington. By the time of the Enlightenment, with its pervading secularism, readers were less shocked by his views. Although these remained of interest to political theorists, the main focus was no longer classical republicanism. That had been replaced by debates over government by contract.

The development of the disciplines of history and politics during the last two centuries has brought about further fluctuations in Machiavelli's reputation. To Jacob Burckhardt, the great Swiss historian of the Renaissance, Machiavelli, despite his dubious morality, was a great thinker, the interpreter *par excellence* of the 'state as a work of art'. Yet other scholars, especially those who concentrated on the views expressed in *The Prince*, found his amorality too much to take. Those, such as Herbert Butterfield, who had experienced two world wars, saw his self-aggrandising programme as a blue-print for how dictators might increase their power. The tendency to conflate personal standards of morality with what Machiavelli was evidently attempting to present as a science of government has always been harmful to his reputation. This was recognised by the authoritative commentator Fedelico Chabod when he wrote that Machiavelli's great contribution to human thought was 'the clear recognition of the autonomy and necessity of politics. Machiavelli thereby rejected the medieval concept of "unity" and became one of the pioneers of the modern spirit.' (*Machiavelli and the Renaissance*, 116)

J. G. A. Pocock, with his concern for the specific language adopted for various forms of political discourse, turned the debate about Machiavelli in a new direction. Quentin Skinner has extended the work, and lays stress on Machiavelli's intellectual heritage and the contemporary context in which he worked. Both scholars have demonstrated that Machiavelli's classical republicanism, when it was combined with newer modes of thought in the seventeenth and eighteenth centuries, had an enduring impact on emergent democracies in Europe and America.

LUCILLE MARGARET KEKEWICH
The Open University

REFERENCES

S. Anglo, *Machiavelli: A Dissection*, Victor Gollancz, London 1969

H. Barron, *The Crisis of the Early Italian Renaissance*, 2 volumes, Princeton University Press 1955

F. Chabod, *Machiavelli and the Renaissance*, trans. D. Moore, Introduction A. P. d'Entrèves, Harper Torchbooks, New York & London 1965

F. Gilbert, *Machiavelli and Guicciardini: Politics and History in Sixteenth Century Florence*, Princeton University Press 1965

C. Grayson (ed.), *Francesco Guicciardini: Selected Writings*, trans. M. Grayson, Oxford University Press 1965

F. Raab, *The English Face of Machiavelli: A Changing Interpretation, 1500-1700*, Routledge and Kegan Paul, London 1964

N. Rubenstein (ed.), *Francesco Guicciardini, Maxims and Reflections of a Renaissance Statesman (Ricordi)*, trans. M. Domandi, Harper Torchbooks, New York & London 1965

Q. Skinner, *The Foundations of Modern Political Thought*, Vol. 1, Cambridge University Press 1978

Q. Skinner, *Machiavelli*, Oxford University Press 1981

Q. Skinner, 'Machiavelli's Discorsi and the pre-humanist origins of republican ideas', *Machiavelli and Republicanism*, ed. G. Bock, Q. Skinner, M. Viroli, pp 121–41, Cambridge University Press 1990

LIST OF EDITIONS USED

The Historical, Political and Diplomatic Writings of Niccolò Machiavelli, trans. C. E. Detmold, 4 vols, Boston 1882. The text of *The Prince* is taken from this edition. Appendix E is an extract from: 'The History of Florence', Vol. 1, Book 8, 36. Appendix B i–iii are extracts from 'Discourses'.

F. Guicciardini, *The History of Florence*, ed. J. R. Hale, trans. C. Grayson, New English Library, London 1966. Appendix A is an extract from Chapter 16.

N. Machiavelli, *The Letters of Machiavelli: A Selection*, ed. and trans. A. Gilbert, Capricorn Books, New York 1961. Appendix C is Letter 137.

Machiavelli: The Chief Works and Others, trans. A. Gilbert, Duke University Press, North Carolina 1965. Appendix D is an extract from 'The Art of War', Vol. 2, Book 1.

Francesco Guicciardini: Selected Writings, ed. C. Grayson, trans. M. Grayson, Oxford University Press 1965. 'Considerations on the *Discourses*'. Appendix F is Chapter 3.

THE PRINCE

NICCOLÒ MACHIAVELLI

TO THE

MAGNIFICENT LORENZO, SON OF PIERO DE' MEDICI

Those who desire to win the favour of princes generally endeavour to do so by offering them those things which they themselves prize most, or such as they observe the prince to delight in most. Thence it is that princes have very often presented to them horses, arms, cloth of gold, precious stones, and similar ornaments worthy of their greatness. Wishing now myself to offer to your Magnificence some proof of my devotion, I have found nothing amongst all I possess that I hold more dear or esteem more highly than the knowledge of the actions of great men, which I have acquired by long experience of modern affairs and a continued study of ancient history.

These I have meditated upon for a long time, and examined with great care and diligence; and having now written them out in a small volume, I send this to your Magnificence. And although I judge this work unworthy of you, yet I trust that your kindness of heart may induce you to accept it, considering that I cannot offer you anything better than the means of understanding in the briefest time all that which I have learnt by so many years of study, and with so much trouble and danger to myself.

I have not set off this little work with pompous phrases, nor filled it with high-sounding and magnificent words, nor with any other allurements or extrinsic embellishments with which many are wont to write and adorn their works; for I wished that mine should derive credit only from the truth of the matter, and that the importance of the subject should make it acceptable.

And I hope it may not be accounted presumption if a man of lowly and humble station ventures to discuss and direct the conduct of princes; for as those who wish to delineate countries place themselves low in the plain to observe the form and character of mountains and high places, and for the purpose of studying the nature of the low country place themselves high upon an eminence, so one must be a prince to know well the character of the people, and to understand well the nature of a prince one must be of the people.

May your Magnificence then accept this little gift in the same spirit in which I send it; and if you will read and consider it well, you will recognise in it my desire that you may attain that greatness which fortune and your great qualities promise. And if your Magnificence will turn your eyes from the summit of your greatness towards those low places, you will know how undeservedly I have to bear the great and continued malice of fortune.

CHAPTER 1

How many kinds of principalities there are, and in what manner they are acquired

All states and governments that have had, and have at present, dominion over men, have been and are either republics or principalities.

The principalities are either hereditary or they are new. Hereditary principalities are those where the government has been for a long time in the family of the prince. New principalities are either entirely new, as was Milan to Francesco Sforza, or they are like appurtenances annexed to the hereditary state of the prince who acquires them, as the kingdom of Naples is to that of Spain.

States thus acquired have been accustomed either to live under a prince, or to exist as free states; and they are acquired either by the arms of others, or by the conqueror's own, or by fortune or valour.

CHAPTER 2

Of hereditary principalities

I will not discuss here the subject of republics, having treated of them at length elsewhere, but will confine myself only to principalities; and following the above indicated order of distinctions, I will proceed to discuss how states of this kind should be governed and maintained. I say, then, that hereditary states, accustomed to the line of their prince, are maintained with much less difficulty than new states. For it is enough merely that the prince do not transcend the order of things established by his predecessors, and that he accommodate himself to events as they occur. So that if such a prince has but ordinary sagacity, he will always maintain himself in his state, unless some extraordinary and superior force should deprive him of it. And even in such a case he will recover it, whenever the occupant meets with any reverses. We have in Italy, for instance, the Duke of Ferrara, who could not have resisted the assaults of the Venetians in 1484, nor those of Pope Julius II in 1510, but for the fact that his family had for a great length of time held the sovereignty of that dominion. For the natural prince has less cause and less necessity for irritating his subjects, whence it is reasonable that he should be more beloved. And unless extraordinary vices should cause him to be hated, he will naturally have the affection of his people. For in the antiquity and continuity of dominion the memory of innovations, and their causes, are effaced; for each change and alteration always prepares the way and facilitates the next.

CHAPTER 3

Of mixed principalities

But it is in a new principality that difficulties present themselves. *[margin note: reflects Henry IV?]* In the first place, if it be not entirely new, but composed of different parts, which when taken all together may as it were be called mixed, its mutations arise in the beginning from a natural difficulty, which is inherent in all new principalities, because men change their rulers gladly, in the belief that they will better themselves by the change. It is this belief that makes them take up arms against the reigning prince; but in this they deceive themselves, for they find afterwards from experience that they have only made their condition worse. *[margin note: unsettled because there is no divine right of kings]* This is the inevitable consequence of another natural and ordinary necessity, which ever obliges a new prince to vex his people with the maintenance of an armed force, and by an infinite number of other wrongs that follow in the train of new conquests. Thus the new prince finds that he has for enemies all those whom he has injured by seizing that principality; and at the same time he cannot preserve as friends even those who have aided him in obtaining possession, because he cannot satisfy their expectations, nor can he employ strong measures against them, being under obligations to them. *[margin note: Problems created for Henry IV]* For however strong a new prince may be in troops, yet will he always have need of the good will of the inhabitants, if he wishes to enter into firm possession of the country.

It was for these reasons that Louis XII, King of France, having suddenly made himself master of Milan, lost it as quickly, Lodovico Sforza's own troops alone having sufficed to wrest it from him the first time. For the very people who had opened the gates to Louis XII, finding themselves deceived in their expectations of immediate as well as prospective advantages, soon became disgusted with the burdens imposed by the new prince.

It is very true that, having recovered such revolted provinces, it is easier to keep them in subjection; for the prince will avail himself of the occasion of the rebellion to secure himself, with less consideration for the people, by punishing the guilty, watching the suspected, and strengthening himself at all the weak points of the province. Thus a mere demonstration on the frontier by Lodovico Sforza lost Milan to the French the first time; but to make them lose it a second time required the whole world to be against them, and that their armies should be dispersed and driven out of Italy; which resulted from the reasons which I have explained above. Nevertheless, France lost Milan both the first and the second time.

The general causes of the first loss have been sufficiently explained; but it remains to be seen now what occasioned the loss of Milan to France the second time, and to point out the remedies which the king had at his command, and which might be employed by any other prince under similar circumstances to maintain himself in a conquered province, but which King Louis XII failed to employ.

I will say then, first, that the states which a prince acquires and annexes to his own dominions are either in the same country, speaking the same language, or they are not. When they are, it is very easy to hold them, especially if they have not been accustomed to govern themselves; for in that case it suffices to extinguish the line of the prince who till then has ruled over them, but otherwise to maintain their old institutions. There being no difference in their manners and customs, the inhabitants will submit quietly, as we have seen in the case of Burgundy, Brittany, Gascony and Normandy, which provinces have remained so long united to France. For although there are some differences of language, yet their customs are similar, and therefore they were easily reconciled to each other. Hence, in order to retain a newly acquired state, regard must be had to two things: one, that the line of the ancient sovereign be entirely extinguished; and the other, that the laws be not changed, nor the taxes increased, so that the new may, in the least possible time, be thoroughly incorporated with the ancient state.

But when states are acquired in a country differing in language, customs, and laws, then come the difficulties, and then it requires great good fortune and much sagacity to hold them; and one of the best and most efficient means is for the prince who has acquired them to go and reside there, which will make his possession more secure and durable. Such was the course adopted by the Turk in Greece, who even if he had respected all the institutions of that country, yet could not possibly have succeeded in holding it, if he had not gone to reside there. For being on the spot, you can quickly remedy disorders as you see them arise; but not being there, you do not hear of them until they have become so great that there is no longer any remedy for them. Besides this, the country will not be despoiled by your officials, and the subjects will be satisfied by the easy recourse to the prince who is near them, which contributes to win their affections, if they are well disposed, and to inspire them with fear, if otherwise. And other powers will hesitate to assail a state where the prince himself resides, as they would find it very difficult to dispossess him.

The next best means for holding a newly acquired state is to establish colonies in one or two places that are as it were the keys to the country. Unless this is done, it will be necessary to keep a large force of men-at-arms and infantry there for its protection. Colonies are not very expensive to the prince; they can be established and maintained at little, if any, cost to him; and only those of the inhabitants will be injured by him whom he deprives of their homes and fields, for the purpose of bestowing them upon the colonists; and this will be the case only with a very small minority of the original inhabitants. And as those who are thus injured by him become dispersed and poor, they can never do him any harm, whilst all the other inhabitants remain on the one hand uninjured, and therefore easily kept quiet, and on the other hand they are afraid to stir, lest they should be despoiled as the others have been. I conclude then that such colonies are inexpensive, and are more faithful to the prince and less injurious to the inhabitants generally; whilst those who are injured by their establishment become poor and dispersed, and therefore unable to do any harm, as I have already said. And here we must observe that men must either be flattered or crushed; for they will revenge themselves for light wrongs, whilst for grave ones they cannot. The injury therefore that you do to a man should be such that you need not fear his revenge.

Henry V going too war would have led to a rebellion.

But if instead of colonies an armed force be sent for the preservation of a newly acquired province, then it will involve much greater expenditures, so that the support of such a guard may consume the entire revenue of the province; so that this acquisition may prove an actual loss, and will moreover give greater offence, because the whole population will feel aggrieved by having the armed force quartered upon them in turn. Every one that is made to suffer from this inconvenience will become an enemy; and these are enemies that can injure the prince, for although beaten yet they remain in their homes. In every point of view, then, such a military guard is disadvantageous, just as colonies are most useful.

A prince, moreover, who wishes to keep possession of a country that is separate and unlike his own, must make himself the chief and protector of the smaller neighbouring powers. He must endeavour to weaken the most powerful of them, and must take care that by no chance a stranger enter that province who is equally powerful with himself; for strangers are never called in except by those whom an undue ambition or fear have rendered malcontents. It was thus in fact that the Aetolians called the Romans into Greece; and whatever other country the Romans entered, it was invariably at the request of the inhabitants.

The way in which these things happen is generally thus: so soon as a powerful foreigner enters a province, all those of its inhabitants that are less powerful will give him their adhesion, being influenced thereto by their jealousy of him who has hitherto been their superior. So that, as regards these petty lords, the new prince need not be at any trouble to win them over to himself, as they will all most readily become incorporated with the state which he has there acquired. He has merely to see to it that they do not assume too much authority, or acquire too much power; for he will then be able by their favour, and by his own strength, very easily to humble those who are really powerful; so that he will in all respects remain the sole arbiter of that province. And he who does not manage this part well will quickly lose what he has acquired; and whilst he holds it, he will experience infinite difficulties and vexations. The Romans observed these points most carefully in the provinces which they conquered; they established colonies there, and sustained the feebler chiefs without increasing their power, whilst they humbled the stronger, and permitted no powerful stranger to acquire any influence or credit there. I will confine myself for an example merely to the provinces of Greece. The Romans sustained the Achaians and the Aetolians, whilst they humbled the kingdom of Macedon and expelled Antiochus from his dominions; but neither the merits of the Achaians nor of the Aetolians caused the Romans to permit either of them to increase in power; nor could the persuasions of Philip induce the Romans to become his friends until after first having humbled his power; nor could the power of Antiochus make them consent that he should hold any state in that province.

Thus in all these cases the Romans did what all wise princes ought to do; namely, not only to look to all present troubles, but also to those of the future, against which they provided with the utmost prudence. For it is by foreseeing difficulties from afar that they are easily provided against; but awaiting their near approach, remedies are no longer in time, for the malady has become incurable. It happens in such cases, as the doctors say of consumption, that in the early stages it is easy to cure, but difficult to recognise; whilst in the course of time, the disease not having been recognised and cured in the beginning, it becomes easy to know, but difficult to cure. And thus it is in the affairs of state; for when the evils that arise in it are seen far ahead, which it is given only to a wise prince to do, then they are easily remedied; but when, in consequence of not having been foreseen, these evils are allowed to grow and assume such proportions that they become manifest to every one, then they can no longer be remedied.

The Romans therefore, on seeing troubles far ahead, always strove to avert them in time, and never permitted their growth merely for the sake of avoiding a war, well knowing that the war would not be prevented, and that to defer it would only be an advantage to others; and for these reasons they resolved upon attacking Philip and Antiochus in Greece, so as to prevent these from making war upon them in Italy. They might at the time have avoided both the one and the other, but would not do it; nor did they ever fancy the saying which is nowadays in the mouth of every wiseacre, 'to bide the advantages of time', but preferred those of their own valour and prudence; for time drives all things before it, and may lead to good as well as to evil, and to evil as well as to good.

But let us return to France, and examine whether she has done any one of the things that we have spoken of. I will say nothing of Charles VIII, but only of Louis XII, whose proceedings we are better able to understand, as he held possession of Italy for a greater length of time. And we shall see how he did the very opposite of what he should have done for the purpose of holding a state so unlike his own.

King Louis XII was called into Italy by the ambition of the Venetians, who wanted him to aid them in conquering a portion of Lombardy. I will not blame the king for the part he took; for, wishing to gain a foothold in Italy, and having no allies there, but rather finding the gates everywhere closed against him in consequence of the conduct of King Charles VIII, he was obliged to avail himself of such friends as he could find; and would have succeeded in his attempt, which was well planned, but for an error which he committed in his subsequent conduct. The king, then, having conquered Lombardy, quickly recovered that reputation which his predecessor, Charles VIII, had lost. Genoa yielded; the Florentines became his friends; the Marquis of Mantua, the Duke of Ferrara, the Bentivogli, the lady of Fourli, the lords of Faenza, Pesaro, Rimini, Camerino and Piombino, the Lucchese, the Pisanese, and the Siennese, all came to meet him with offers of friendship. The Venetians might then have recognised the folly of their course, when, for the sake of gaining two cities in Lombardy, they made King Louis master of two thirds of Italy.

Let us see now how easily the king might have maintained his influence in Italy if he had observed the rules above given. Had he secured and protected all these friends of his, who were numerous but feeble – some fearing the Church, and some the Venetians, and therefore all forced to adhere to him – he might easily have secured himself against the remaining stronger powers of Italy. But no sooner in Milan than he did the very opposite, by giving aid to Pope Alexander VI to enable him to seize the Romagna. Nor did he perceive that in doing this he weakened himself, by alienating his friends and those who had thrown themselves into his arms; and that he had made the Church great by adding so much temporal to its spiritual power, which gave it already so much authority. Having committed this first error, he was obliged to follow it up; so that, for the purpose of putting an end to the ambition of Pope Alexander VI, and preventing his becoming master of Tuscany, he was obliged to come into Italy.

Not content with having made the Church great, and with having alienated his own friends, King Louis, in his eagerness to possess the kingdom of Naples, shared it with the king of Spain; so that where he had been the sole arbiter of Italy, he established an associate and rival, to whom the ambitious and the malcontents might have a ready recourse. And whilst he could have left a king in Naples who would have been his tributary, he dispossessed him, for the sake of replacing him by another who was powerful enough in turn to drive him out.

The desire of conquest is certainly most natural and common amongst men, and whenever they yield to it and are successful, they are praised; but when they lack the means, and yet attempt it anyhow, then they commit an error that merits blame. If, then, the king of France was powerful enough by himself successfully to attack the kingdom of Naples, then he was right to do so; but if he was not, then he should not have divided it with the king of Spain. And if the partition of Lombardy with the Venetians was excusable because it enabled him to gain a foothold in Italy, that of Naples with the Spaniard deserves censure, as it cannot be excused on the ground of necessity.

Louis XII then committed these five errors: he destroyed the weak; he increased the power of one already powerful in Italy; he established a most powerful stranger there; he did not go to reside there himself; nor did he plant any colonies there. These errors, however, would not have injured him during his lifetime, had he not committed a sixth one in attempting to deprive the Venetians of their possessions. For if Louis had not increased the power of the Church, nor established the Spaniards in Italy, it would have been quite reasonable, and even advisable, for him to have weakened the Venetians; but having done both those things, he ought never to have consented to their ruin; for so long as the Venetians were powerful, they would always have kept others from any attempt upon Lombardy. They would on the one hand never have permitted this unless it should have led to their becoming masters of it, and on the other hand no one would have taken it from France for the sake of giving it to the Venetians; nor would any one have had the courage to attack the French and the Venetians combined. And should it be said that King Louis gave up the Romagna to Pope Alexander VI, and divided the kingdom of Naples with the Spaniard, for the sake of avoiding a war, then I reply with the above stated reasons, that no one should ever submit to an evil for the sake of avoiding a war. For a war is never avoided, but is only deferred to one's own disadvantage.

And should it be argued, on the other hand, that the king felt bound by the pledge which he had given to the Pope to conquer the Romagna for him in consideration of his dissolving the king's marriage, and of his bestowing the cardinal's hat upon the Archbishop of Rouen, then I meet that argument with what I shall say further on concerning the pledges of princes, and the manner in which they should keep them.

King Louis then lost Lombardy by not having conformed to any one of the conditions that have been observed by others who, having conquered provinces, wanted to keep them. Nor is this at all to be wondered at, for it is quite reasonable and common. I conversed on this subject with the Archbishop of Rouen (Cardinal d'Amboise) whilst at Nantes, when the Duke Valentino, commonly called Cesare Borgia, son of Pope Alexander VI, made himself master of the Romagna. On that occasion the Cardinal said to me, that the Italians did not understand the art of war. To which I replied that the French did not understand statesmanship; for if they had understood it, they would never have allowed the Church to attain such greatness and power. For experience proves that the greatness of the Church and that of Spain in Italy were brought about by France, and that her own ruin resulted therefrom. From this we draw the general rule, which never or rarely fails, that the prince who causes another to become powerful thereby works his own ruin; for he has contributed to the power of the other either by his own ability or force, and both the one and the other will be mistrusted by him whom he has thus made powerful.

CHAPTER 4

*Why the kingdom of Darius, which was
conquered by Alexander, did not revolt against
the successors of Alexander after his death*

If we reflect upon the difficulties of preserving a newly acquired
state, it seems marvellous that after the rapid conquest of all Asia
by Alexander the Great, and his subsequent death, which one
would suppose most naturally to have provoked the whole
country to revolt, yet his successors maintained their possession of
it, and experienced no other difficulties in holding it than such as
arose amongst themselves from their own ambition.

I meet this observation by saying that all principalities of which
we have any accounts have been governed in one of two ways;
viz. either by one absolute prince, to whom all others are as slaves,
some of whom, as ministers, by his grace and consent aid him in
the government of his realm; or else by a prince and nobles, who
hold that rank, not by the grace of their sovereign, but by the
antiquity of their lineage. Such nobles have estates and subjects of
their own, who recognise them as their liege lords, and have a
natural affection for them.

In those states that are governed by an absolute prince and slaves,
the prince has far more power and authority; for in his entire
dominion no one recognises any other superior but him; and if they
obey any one else, they do it as though to his minister and officer,
and without any particular affection for such official. Turkey and
France furnish us examples of these two different systems of
government at the present time. The whole country of the Turk is
governed by one master; all the rest are his slaves; and having
divided the country into Sanjacs, or districts, he appoints governors
for each of these, whom he changes and replaces at his pleasure.

But the king of France is placed in the midst of a large number of ancient nobles, who are recognised and acknowledged by their subjects as their lords, and are held in great affection by them. They have their rank and prerogatives, of which the king cannot deprive them without danger to himself. In observing now these two principalities, we perceive the difficulty of conquering the empire of the Turk, but once conquered it will be very easily held. The reasons that make the conquest of the Turkish empire so difficult are, that the conqueror cannot be called into the country by any of the great nobles of the state; nor can he hope that his attempt could be facilitated by a revolt of those who surround the sovereign; which arises from the above given reasons. For being all slaves and dependants of their sovereign, it is more difficult to corrupt them; and even if they were corrupted, but little advantage could be hoped for from them, because they cannot carry the people along with them.

Whoever therefore attacks the Turks must expect to find them united, and must depend wholly upon his own forces, and not upon any internal disturbances. But once having defeated and driven the Turk from the field, so that he cannot reorganise his army, then he will have nothing to fear but the line of the sovereign. This however once extinguished, the conqueror has nothing to apprehend from any one else, as none other has any influence with the people; and thus, having had nothing to hope from them before the victory, he will have nothing to fear from them afterwards.

The contrary takes place in kingdoms governed like that of France; for having gained over some of the great nobles of the realm, there will be no difficulty in entering it, there being always malcontents and others who desire a change. These, for the reasons stated, can open the way into the country for the assailant, and facilitate his success. But for the conqueror to maintain himself there afterwards will involve infinite difficulties, both with the conquered and with those who have aided him in his conquest. Nor will it suffice to extinguish the line of the sovereign, because the great nobles remain, who will place themselves at the head of new movements; and the conqueror, not being able either to satisfy or to crush them, will lose the country again on the first occasion that presents itself.

If now we consider the nature of the government of Darius [of Persia], we shall find that it resembled that of the Turk, and therefore it was necessary for Alexander to attack him in full force, and drive him from the field. After this victory and the death of Darius, Alexander remained in secure possession of the kingdom for the reasons above explained. And if his successors had remained united, they might also have enjoyed possession at their ease; for no other disturbances occurred in that empire, except such as they created themselves.

Countries, however, with a system of government like that of France, cannot possibly be held so easily. The frequent insurrections of Spain, France, and Greece against the Romans were due to the many petty princes that existed in those states; and therefore, so long as the memory of these princes endured, the Romans were ever uncertain in the tenure of those states. But all remembrance of these princes once effaced, the Romans became secure possessors of those countries, so long as the growth and power of their empire endured. And even afterwards, when fighting amongst themselves, each of the parties were able to keep for themselves portions of those countries, according to the authority which they had acquired there; and the line of their sovereigns being extinguished, the inhabitants recognised no other authority but that of the Romans.

Reflecting now upon these things, we cannot be surprised at the facility with which Alexander maintained himself in Asia; nor at the difficulties which others experienced in preserving their conquests, as was the case with Pyrrhus and many others, and which resulted not from the greater or lesser valour of the conqueror, but from the different nature of the conquered states.

CHAPTER 5

*How cities or principalities are to be governed
that previous to being conquered had
lived under their own laws*

Conquered states that have been accustomed to liberty and the government of their own laws can be held by the conqueror in three different ways. The first is to ruin them; the second, for the conqueror to go and reside there in person; and the third is to allow them to continue to live under their own laws, subject to a regular tribute, and to create in them a government of a few, who will keep the country friendly to the conqueror. Such a government, having been established by the new prince, knows that it cannot maintain itself without the support of his power and friendship, and it becomes its interest therefore to sustain him. A city that has been accustomed to free institutions is much easier held by its own citizens than in any other way, if the conqueror desires to preserve it. The Spartans and the Romans will serve as examples of these different ways of holding a conquered state.

The Spartans held Athens and Thebes, creating there a government of a few; and yet they lost both these states again. The Romans, for the purpose of retaining Capua, Carthage, and Numantia, destroyed them, but did not lose them. They wished to preserve Greece in somewhat the same way that the Spartans had held it, by making her free and leaving her in the enjoyment of her own laws, but did not succeed; so that they were obliged to destroy many cities in that country for the purpose of holding it. In truth there was no other safe way of keeping possession of that country but to ruin it. And whoever becomes master of a city that has been accustomed to liberty, and does not destroy it, must himself expect to be ruined by it. For they will always resort to rebellion in the name of liberty and their ancient institutions, which will never be effaced from their memory, either by the lapse of time, or by benefits bestowed by the new master. No matter what he may do, or what precautions he may take, if he does not separate and disperse the inhabitants, they will on the first occasion invoke the name of liberty and the memory of their ancient institutions, as was done by Pisa after having been held over a hundred years in subjection by the Florentines.

But it is very different with states that have been accustomed to live under a prince. When the line of the prince is once extinguished, the inhabitants, being on the one hand accustomed to obey, and on the other having lost their ancient sovereign, can neither agree to create a new one from amongst themselves, nor do they know how to live in liberty; and thus they will be less prompt to take up arms, and the new prince will readily be able to gain their good will and to assure himself of them. But republics have more vitality, a greater spirit of resentment and desire of revenge, for the memory of their ancient liberty neither can nor will permit them to remain quiet, and therefore the surest way of holding them is either to destroy them, or for the conqueror to go and live there.

CHAPTER 6

*Of new principalities that have been acquired by
the valour of the prince and by his own troops*

Let no one wonder if, in what I am about to say of entirely new
principalities and of the prince and his government, I cite the very
highest examples. For as men almost always follow the beaten
track of others, and proceed in their actions by imitation, and yet
cannot altogether follow the ways of others, nor attain the high
qualities of those whom they imitate, so a wise man should ever
follow the ways of great men and endeavour to imitate only such
as have been most eminent; so that even if his merits do not quite
equal theirs, yet that they may in some measure reflect their
greatness. He should do as the skilful archer, who, seeing that the
object he desires to hit is too distant, and knowing the extent to
which his bow will carry, aims higher than the destined mark, not
for the purpose of sending his arrow to that height, but so that by
this elevation it may reach the desired aim.

I say then that a new prince in an entirely new principality will
experience more or less difficulty in maintaining himself,
according as he has more or less courage and ability. And as such
an event as to become a prince from a mere private individual
presupposes either great courage or rare good fortune, it would
seem that one or the other of these two causes ought in a measure
to mitigate many of these difficulties. But he who depends least
upon fortune will maintain himself best; which will be still more
easy for the Prince if, having no other state, he is obliged to reside
in his newly acquired principality.

To come now to those who by their courage and ability, and
not by fortune, have risen to the rank of rulers, I will say that the
most eminent of such were Moses, Cyrus, Romulus, Theseus and

the like. And although we may not discuss Moses, who was a mere executor of the things ordained by God, yet he merits our admiration, if only for that grace which made him worthy to hold direct communion with the Almighty. But if we consider Cyrus and others who have conquered or founded empires, we shall find them all worthy of admiration; for if we study their acts and particular ordinances, they do not seem very different from those of Moses, although he had so great a teacher. We shall also find in examining their acts and lives, that they had no other favour from fortune but opportunity, which gave them the material which they could mould into whatever form seemed to them best; and without such opportunity the great qualities of their souls would have been wasted, whilst without those great qualities the opportunities would have been in vain.

It was necessary then for Moses to find the people of Israel slaves in Egypt, and oppressed by the Egyptians, so that to escape from that bondage they resolved to follow him. It was necessary that Romulus should not have been kept in Alba, and that he should have been exposed at his birth, for him to have become the founder and king of Rome. And so it was necessary for Cyrus to find the Persians dissatisfied with the rule of the Medes, and the Medes effeminate and enfeebled by long peace. And finally, Theseus could not have manifested his courage had he not found the Athenians dispersed. These opportunities therefore made these men fortunate, and it was their lofty virtue that enabled them to recognise the opportunities by which their countries were made illustrious and most happy. Those who by similar noble conduct become princes acquire their principalities with difficulty, but maintain them with ease; and the difficulties which they experience in acquiring their principalities arise in part from the new ordinances and customs which they are obliged to introduce for the purpose of founding their state and their own security. We must bear in mind, then, that there is nothing more difficult and dangerous, or more doubtful of success, than an attempt to introduce a new order of things in any state. For the innovator has for enemies all those who derived advantages from the old order of things, whilst those who expect to be benefited by the new institutions will be but lukewarm defenders. This indifference arises in part from fear of their adversaries who were favoured by the existing laws, and partly from the incredulity of men who have no faith in anything new that is not the result of well-established experience. Hence it is that, whenever the opponents of the new order of things have the opportunity to attack it, they will do it with the zeal of partisans, whilst the others defend it but feebly, so that it is dangerous to rely upon the latter.

If we desire to discuss this subject thoroughly, it will be necessary to examine whether such innovators depend upon themselves, or whether they rely upon others; that is to say, whether for the purpose of carrying out their plans they have to resort to entreaties, or whether they can accomplish it by force. In the first case they always succeed badly, and fail to conclude anything; but when they depend upon their own strength to carry their innovations through, then they rarely incur any danger. Thence it was that all prophets who came with arms in hand were successful, whilst those who were not armed were ruined. For besides the reasons given above, the dispositions of peoples are variable; it is easy to persuade them to anything, but difficult to confirm them in that belief. And therefore a prophet should be prepared, in case the people will not believe any more, to be able by force to compel them to that belief.

Neither Moses, Cyrus, Theseus, nor Romulus would have been able to make their laws and institutions observed for any length of time, if they had not been prepared to enforce them with arms. This was the experience of Brother Girolamo Savonarola, who failed in his attempt to establish a new order of things so soon as the multitude ceased to believe in him; for he had not the means to keep his believers firm in their faith, nor to make the unbelievers believe. And yet these great men experienced great difficulties in their course, and met danger at every step, which could only be overcome by their courage and ability. But once having surmounted them, then they began to be held in veneration; and having crushed those who were jealous of their great qualities, they remained powerful, secure, honoured and happy.

To these great examples I will add a minor one, which nevertheless bears some relation to them, and will suffice me for all similar cases. This is Hiero of Syracuse, who from a mere private individual rose to be prince of Syracuse, although he owed no other favour to fortune than opportunity; for the Syracusans, being oppressed, elected him their captain, whence he advanced by his merits to become their prince. And even in his condition as a private citizen he displayed such virtue, that the author who wrote of him said that he lacked nothing of being a monarch excepting a kingdom. Hiero disbanded the old army and organised a new one; he abandoned his old allies and formed new alliances; and having thus an army and allies of his own creation, he had no difficulty in erecting any edifice upon such a foundation; so that although he had much trouble in attaining the principality, yet he had but little in maintaining it.

CHAPTER 7

Of new principalities that have been acquired by the aid of others and by good fortune

Those who by good fortune only rise from mere private station to the dignity of princes have but little trouble in achieving that elevation, for they fly there as it were on wings; but their difficulties begin after they have been placed in that high position. Such are those who acquire a state either by means of money, or by the favour of some powerful monarch who bestows it upon them. Many such instances occurred in Greece, in the cities of Ionia and of the Hellespont, where men were made princes by Darius so that they might hold those places for his security and glory. And such were those emperors who from having been mere private individuals attained the empire by corrupting the soldiery. These remain simply subject to the will and the fortune of those who bestowed greatness upon them, which are two most uncertain and variable things. And generally these men have neither the skill nor the power to maintain that high rank. They know not (for unless they are men of great genius and ability, it is not reasonable that they should know) how to command, having never occupied any but private stations; and they cannot, because they have no troops upon whose loyalty and attachment they can depend.

Moreover, states that spring up suddenly, like other things in nature that are born and attain their growth rapidly, cannot have those roots and supports that will protect them from destruction by the first unfavourable weather. Unless indeed, as has been said, those who have suddenly become princes are gifted with such ability that they quickly know how to prepare themselves for the preservation of that which fortune has cast into their lap, and afterwards to build up those foundations which others have laid before becoming princes.

In illustration of the one and the other of these two ways of becoming princes, by valour and ability, or by good fortune, I will adduce two examples from the time within our own memory; these are Francesco Sforza and Cesare Borgia. Francesco, by legitimate means and by great natural ability, rose from a private citizen to be Duke of Milan; and having attained that high position by a thousand efforts, it cost him but little trouble afterwards to maintain it. On the other hand, Cesare Borgia, commonly called Duke Valentino, acquired his state by the good fortune of his father, but lost it when no longer sustained by that good fortune; although he employed all the means and did all that a brave and prudent man can do to take root in that state which had been bestowed upon him by the arms and good fortune of another. For, as we have said above, he who does not lay the foundations for his power beforehand may be able by great ability and courage to do so afterwards; but it will be done with great trouble to the builder and with danger to the edifice.

If now we consider the whole course of the Duke Valentino, we shall see that he took pains to lay solid foundations for his future power; which I think it well to discuss. For I should not know what better lesson I could give to a new prince, than to hold up to him the example of the Duke Valentino's conduct. And if the measures which he adopted did not insure his final success, the fault was not his, for his failure was due to the extreme and extraordinary malignity of fortune. Pope Alexander VI in his efforts to aggrandise his son, the Duke Valentino, encountered many difficulties, immediate and prospective. In the first place he saw that there was no chance of making him master of any state, unless a state of the Church; and he knew that neither the Duke of Milan nor the Venetians would consent to that. Faenza and Rimini were already at that time under the protection of the Venetians; and the armies of Italy, especially those of which he could have availed himself, were in the hands of men who had cause to fear the power of the Pope, namely the Orsini, the Colonna [two noble Roman families] and their adherents; and therefore he could not rely upon them.

It became necessary therefore for Alexander to disturb the

existing order of things, and to disorganise those states, in order to make himself safely master of them. And this it was easy for him to do; for he found the Venetians, influenced by other reasons, favourable to the return of the French into Italy; which not only he did not oppose, but facilitated by dissolving the former marriage of King Louis XII (so as to enable him to marry Ann of Brittany). The king thereupon entered Italy with the aid of the Venetians and the consent of Alexander; and no sooner was he in Milan than the Pope obtained troops from him to aid in the conquest of the Romagna, which was yielded to him through the influence of the king.

The Duke Valentino having thus acquired the Romagna, and the Colonna being discouraged, he both wished to hold that province, and also to push his possessions still further, but was prevented by two circumstances. The one was that his own troops seemed to him not to be reliable, and the other was the will of the king of France. That is to say, he feared lest the Orsini troops, which he had made use of, might fail him at the critical moment, and not only prevent him from acquiring more, but even take from him that which he had acquired; and that even the king of France might do the same. Of the disposition of the Orsini, the duke had a proof when, after the capture of Faenza, he attacked Bologna, and saw with what indifference they moved to the assault. And as to the king of France, he knew his mind; for when he wanted to march into Tuscany, after having taken the Duchy of Urbino, King Louis made him desist from that undertaking. The duke resolved therefore to rely no longer upon the fortune or the arms of others. And the first thing he did was to weaken the Orsini and the Colonna in Rome, by winning over to himself all the gentlemen adherents of those houses, by taking them into his own pay as gentlemen followers, giving them liberal stipends and bestowing honours upon them in proportion to their condition, and giving them appointments and commands; so that in the course of a few months their attachment to their factions was extinguished, and they all became devoted followers of the duke.

After that, having successfully dispersed the Colonna faction, he watched for an opportunity to crush the Orsini, which soon presented itself, and of which he made the most. For the Orsini, having been slow to perceive that the aggrandisement of the duke and of the Church would prove the cause of their ruin, convened a meeting at Magione, in the Perugine territory, which gave rise to the revolt of Urbino and the disturbances in the Romagna, and caused infinite dangers to the Duke Valentino, all of which, however, he overcame with the aid of the French. Having thus re-established his reputation, and trusting no longer in the French or any other foreign power, he had recourse to deceit, so as to avoid putting them to the test. And so well did he know how to dissemble and conceal his intentions that the Orsini became reconciled to him, through the agency of the Signor Paolo, whom the duke had won over to himself by means of all possible good offices, and gifts of money, clothing, and horses. And thus their credulity led them into the hands of the duke at Sinigaglia.

The chiefs thus destroyed, and their adherents converted into his friends, the duke had laid sufficiently good foundations for his power, having made himself master of the whole of the Romagna and the Duchy of Urbino, and having attached their entire population to himself, by giving them a foretaste of the new prosperity which they were to enjoy under him. And as this part of the duke's proceedings is well worthy of notice and may serve as an example to others, I will dwell upon it more fully.

Having conquered the Romagna, the duke found it under the control of a number of impotent petty tyrants, who had devoted themselves more to plundering their subjects than to governing them properly, and encouraging discord and disorder amongst them rather than peace and union; so that this province was infested by brigands, torn by quarrels, and given over to every sort of violence. He saw at once that, to restore order amongst the inhabitants and obedience to the sovereign, it was necessary to establish a good and vigorous government there. And for this purpose he appointed as governor of that province Don Ramiro d' Orco, a man of cruelty, but at the same time of great energy, to whom he gave plenary power. In a very short time d'Orco reduced the province to peace and order, thereby gaining for him the highest reputation. After a while the duke found such excessive exercise of authority no longer necessary or expedient, for he feared that it might render himself odious. He therefore established a civil tribunal in the heart of the province, under an excellent president, where every city should have its own advocate. And having observed that the past rigour of Ramiro had engendered some hatred, he wished to show to the people, for the purpose of removing that feeling from their minds, and to win their entire confidence, that if any cruelties had been practised, they had not originated with him, but had resulted altogether from the harsh nature of his minister. He therefore took occasion to have Messer Ramiro put to death, and his body, cut into two parts, exposed in the market-place of Cesena one morning, with a block of wood and a bloody cutlass left beside him. The horror of this spectacle caused the people to remain for a time stupefied and satisfied.

But let us return to where we started from. I say, then, that the duke, feeling himself strong enough now, and in a measure secure from immediate danger, having raised an armed force of his own, and having in great part destroyed those that were near and might have troubled him, wanted now to proceed with his conquest. The only power remaining which he had to fear was the king of France, upon whose support he knew that he could not count, although the king had been late in discovering his error of having allowed the duke's aggrandisement. The duke, therefore, began to look for new alliances, and to prevaricate with the French about their entering the kingdom of Naples for the purpose of attacking the Spaniards, who were then engaged in the siege of Gaeta. His intention was to place them in such a position that they would not be able to harm him; and in this he would have succeeded easily if Pope Alexander had lived.

Such was the course of the Duke Valentino with regard to the immediate present, but he had cause for apprehensions as to the future; mainly, lest the new successor to the papal chair should not be friendly to him, and should attempt to take from him what had been given him by Alexander. And this he thought of preventing in several different ways: one, by extirpating the families of those whom he had despoiled, so as to deprive the Pope of all pretext of restoring them to their possessions; secondly, by gaining over to himself all the gentlemen of Rome, so as to be able, through them, to keep the Pope in check; thirdly, by getting the College of Cardinals under his control; and, fourthly, by acquiring so much power before the death of Alexander that he might by himself be able to resist the first attack of his enemies. Of these four things he had accomplished three at the time of Alexander's death; for of the petty tyrants whom he had despoiled he had killed as many as he could lay hands on, and but very few had been able to save themselves; he had won over to himself the gentlemen of Rome, and had secured a large majority in the sacred college; and as to further acquisitions, he contemplated making himself master of Tuscany, having already possession of Perugia and Piombino, and having assumed a protectorate over Pisa. There being no longer occasion to be apprehensive of France, which had been deprived of the kingdom of Naples by the Spaniards, so that both of these powers had to seek his friendship, he suddenly seized Pisa. After this, Lucca and Siena promptly yielded to him, partly from jealousy of the Florentines and partly from fear. Thus Florence saw no safety from the duke, and if he had succeeded in taking that city, as he could have done in the very year of Alexander's death, it would have so increased his power and influence that he would have been able to have sustained himself alone, without depending upon the fortune or power of any one else, and relying solely upon his own strength and courage.

But Alexander died five years after the duke had first unsheathed his sword. He left his son with only his government of the Romagna firmly established, but all his other possessions entirely uncertain, hemmed in between two powerful hostile armies, and himself sick unto death. But such were the duke's energy and courage, and so well did he know how men are either won or destroyed, and so solid were the foundations which he had in so brief a time laid for his greatness, that if he had not had these two armies upon his back, and had been in health, he would have sustained himself against all difficulties. And that the foundations of his power were well laid may be judged by the fact that the Romagna remained faithful, and waited quietly for him more than a month; and that, although half dead with sickness, yet he was perfectly secure in Rome; and that, although the Baglioni, Vitelli and Orsini came to Rome at the time, yet they could not raise a party against him. Unable to make a Pope of his own choice, yet he could prevent the election of any one that was not acceptable to him. And had the duke been in health at the time of Alexander's death, everything would have gone well with him;

for he said to me on the day when Julius II was created Pope, that he had provided for everything that could possibly occur in case of his father's death, except that he never thought that at that moment he should himself be so near dying.

Upon reviewing now all the actions of the duke, I should not know where to blame him; it seems to me that I should rather hold him up as an example (as I have said) to be imitated by all those who have risen to sovereignty, either by the good fortune or the arms of others. For being endowed with great courage, and having a lofty ambition, he could not have acted otherwise under the circumstances; and the only thing that defeated his designs was the shortness of Alexander's life and his own bodily infirmity.

Whoever, then, in a newly acquired state, finds it necessary to secure himself against his enemies, to gain friends, to conquer by force or by cunning, to make himself feared or beloved by the people, to be followed and revered by the soldiery, to destroy all who could or might injure him, to substitute a new for the old order of things, to be severe and yet gracious, magnanimous and liberal, to disband a disloyal army and create a new one, to preserve the friendship of kings and princes, so that they may bestow benefits upon him with grace, and fear to injure him – such a one, I say, cannot find more recent examples than those presented by the conduct of the Duke Valentino. The only thing we can blame him for was the election of Julius II to the Pontificate, which was a bad selection for him to make; for, as has been said, though he was not able to make a Pope to his own liking, yet he could have prevented, and should never have consented to, the election of one from amongst those cardinals whom he had offended, or who, if he had been elected, would have had occasion to fear him, for either fear or resentment makes men enemies.

Those whom the duke had offended were, amongst others, the Cardinals San Pietro ad Vincola [afterwards Julius II], Colonna, San Giorgio, and Ascanio. All the others, had they come to the pontificate, would have had to fear him, excepting D'Amboise and the Spanish cardinals; the latter because of certain relations and reciprocal obligations, and the former because of his power, he having France for his ally. The duke then should by all means have had one of the Spanish cardinals made Pope, and failing in that, he should have supported the election of the Cardinal d'Amboise, and not that of the Cardinal San Pietro in Vincola. For whoever thinks that amongst great personages recent benefits will cause old injuries to be forgotten, deceives himself greatly. The duke, then, in consenting to the election of Julius II, committed an error which proved the cause of his ultimate ruin.

CHAPTER 8

Of such as have achieved sovereignty by means of crimes

But as there are also two ways in which a person may rise from private station to sovereignty, and which can neither be attributed to fortune nor to valour, it seems to me they should not be left unnoticed; although one of these ways might be more fully discussed when we treat of republics. These two modes are, when one achieves sovereignty either by wicked and nefarious means, or when a private citizen becomes sovereign of his country by the favour of his fellow-citizens. I will explain the first by two examples, the one ancient and the other modern; and without entering otherwise into the merits of these cases, I judge they will suffice to any one who may find himself obliged to imitate them.

Agathocles, a Sicilian, rose to be king of Syracuse, not only from being a mere private citizen, but from the lowest and most abject condition. He was the son of a potter, and led a vicious life through all the various phases of his career. But his wickedness was coupled with so much moral and physical courage, that, having joined the army, he rose by successive steps until he became Praetor of Syracuse. Having attained that rank he resolved to make himself sovereign, and to retain by violence, and regardless of others, that which had been entrusted to him by public consent. For this purpose he came to an understanding with Hamilcar the Carthaginian, who was at that time carrying on war with his army in Sicily; and having one morning called an assembly of the people and the Senate of Syracuse, as though he wished to confer with them about public affairs, he made his soldiers, at a given signal, slay all the Senators and the richest of the people, and then seized the sovereignty of that city without any resistance on the part of the citizens. Although afterwards twice defeated by the Carthaginians, and finally besieged by them in Syracuse, he not only defended that city, but, leaving a portion of his forces to sustain the siege, he crossed the sea with the other part and attacked Africa, thus raising the siege of Syracuse in a short time, and driving the Carthaginians to the extremest necessity, compelling them to make terms with him, and to remain content with the possession of Africa, and leave Sicily to him.

Whoever now reflects upon the conduct and valour of Agathocles will find in them little or nothing that can be attributed to fortune; for, as I have said, he achieved sovereignty, not by the favour of any one, but through his high rank in the army, which he had won by a thousand efforts and dangers, and he afterwards maintained his sovereignty with great courage, and even temerity. And yet we cannot call it valour to massacre one's fellow-citizens, to betray one's friends, and to be devoid of good faith, mercy, and religion; such means may enable a man to achieve empire, but not glory. Still, if we consider the valour of Agathocles in encountering and overcoming dangers, and his invincible courage in supporting and mastering adversity, we shall find no reason why he should be regarded inferior to any of the most celebrated captains. But with all this, his outrageous cruelty and inhumanity, together with his infinite crimes, will not permit him to be classed with the most celebrated men. We cannot therefore ascribe to either valour or fortune the achievements of Agathocles, which he accomplished without either the one or the other.

In our own times, during the pontificate of Alexander VI, Oliverotto da Fermo, having been left an orphan, was brought up by his maternal uncle, Giovanni Fogliani, and was in early youth placed in the military service under Paolo Vitelli; so that, after having been thoroughly trained and disciplined, he might attain prominent rank in the army. After the death of Paolo, he served under his brother Vitellozzo; and became in a very short time, by his intelligence, his bodily strength and intrepidity, one of the foremost men in his service. But deeming it servile to act under the command of others, he planned, together with some of the citizens of Fermo who preferred servitude to the liberty of their country, and with the concurrence of Vitellozzo, to seize Fermo and make himself lord of the same. With this object he wrote to his uncle, Giovanni Fogliani, that, having been absent from home for several years, he desired now to come to see him and his native city, and also to look up his patrimony; and that, having until then striven only to acquire honour, he desired to show his fellow-citizens that he had not laboured in vain; and therefore he wished to come in splendid style, accompanied by one hundred cavaliers, friends of his. He begged his uncle, therefore, to be pleased to arrange that the inhabitants of Fermo should give him an honourable reception, which would be an honour not only to him, but also to Giovanni, who was his near relative and had brought him up. Giovanni therefore omitted no courtesies due to his nephew, and caused the citizens of Fermo to give him an honourable reception, as well as lodgings in their houses for himself and all his retinue. After spending some days in Fermo, and arranging all that was necessary for the execution of his villainous design, Oliverotto gave a sumptuous entertainment, to which he invited his uncle Giovanni and all the principal citizens of Fermo. After the dinner and the other entertainments that are customary on such occasions, Oliverotto artfully started a grave discussion respecting the greatness of Pope Alexander VI and his son Cesare Borgia and their enterprises. When Giovanni and the others replied to his remarks, Oliverotto suddenly arose, saying that these things were only to be spoken of in private places, and withdrew to another room, whither Giovanni and the other citizens followed. No sooner had they seated themselves there, than some of Oliverotto's soldiers rushed out from concealment and massacred Giovanni and all the others.

After this murder Oliverotto mounted his horse, rode through the streets of Fermo, and besieged the supreme magistrates in the palace, who, constrained by fear, obeyed him, and formed a government of which Oliverotto made himself sovereign. And as all those who, as malcontents, might have injured him, had been put to death, Oliverotto fortified himself in his position with new institutions, both civil and military, so that for the space of a year, during which he held the sovereignty, he was not only secure in the city of Fermo, but had become formidable to all his neighbours; so that it would have been as difficult to overcome him as Agathocles, had he not allowed himself to be deceived by Cesare Borgia, when, as I have related, he entrapped the Orsini and the Vitelli at Sinigaglia, where Oliverotto was also taken and strangled, together with Vitellozzo, his master in valour and in villainy, just one year after he had committed parricide in having his uncle Giovanni Fogliani assassinated.

Some may wonder how it was that Agathocles, and others like him, after their infinite treason and cruelty, could live for any length of time securely in the countries whose sovereignty they had usurped, and even defend themselves successfully against external enemies, without any attempts on the part of their own citizens to conspire against them; whilst many others could not by means of cruelty maintain their state even in time of peace, much less in doubtful times of war. I believe that this happened according as the cruelties were well or ill applied; we may call cruelty well applied (if indeed we may call that well which in itself is evil) when it is committed once from necessity for self-protection, and afterwards not persisted in, but converted as far as possible to the public good. Ill-applied cruelties are those which, though at first but few, yet increase with time rather than cease altogether. Those who adopt the first practice may, with the help of God and man, render some service to their state, as had been done by Agathocles; but those who adopt the latter course will not possibly be able to maintain themselves in their state. Whence it is to be noted that in taking possession of a state the conqueror should well reflect as to the harsh measures that may be necessary, and then execute them at a single blow, so as not to be obliged to renew them every day; and by thus not repeating them, to assure himself of the support of the inhabitants, and win them over to himself by benefits bestowed. And he who acts otherwise, either from timidity or from being badly advised, will be obliged ever to be sword in hand, and will never be able to rely upon his subjects, who in turn will not be able to rely upon him, because of the constant fresh wrongs committed by him. Cruelties should be committed all at once, as in that way each separate one is less felt, and gives less offence; benefits, on the other hand, should be conferred one at a time, for in that way they will be more appreciated. But above all a prince should live upon such terms with his subjects that no accident, either for good or for evil, should make him vary his conduct towards them. For when adverse times bring upon you the necessity for action, you will no longer be in time to do evil; and the good you may do will not profit you, because it will be regarded as having been forced from you, and therefore will bring you no thanks.

CHAPTER 9

Of civil principalities

But let us come now to that other case, when a prominent citizen has become prince of his country, not by treason and violence, but by the favour of his fellow-citizens. This may be called a civil principality; and to attain it requires neither great virtue nor extraordinary good fortune, but rather a happy shrewdness. I say, then, that such principalities are achieved either by the favour of the people or by that of the nobles; for in every state there will be found two different dispositions, which result from this – that the people dislike being ruled and oppressed by the nobles, whilst the nobles seek to rule and oppress the people. And this diversity of feeling and interests engenders one of three effects in a state: these are either a principality, or a government of liberty, or licence. A principality results either from the will of the people or from that of the nobles, according as either the one or the other prevails and has the opportunity. For the nobles, seeing that they cannot resist the people, begin to have recourse to the influence and reputation of one of their own class, and make him a prince, so that under the shadow of his power they may give free scope to their desires. The people also, seeing that they cannot resist the nobles, have recourse to the influence and reputation of one man, and make him prince, so as to be protected by his authority. He who becomes prince by the aid of the nobles will have more difficulty in maintaining himself than he who arrives at that high station by the aid of the people. For the former finds himself surrounded by many who in their own opinion are equal to him, and for that reason he can neither command nor manage them in his own way. But he who attains the principality by favour of the people stands alone, and has around him none, or very few, that will not yield him a ready obedience. Moreover, you cannot satisfy the nobles with honesty, and without wrong to others, but it is easy to satisfy the people, whose aims are ever more honest than those of the nobles; the latter wishing to oppress, and the former being unwilling to be oppressed. I will say further, that a prince can never assure himself of a people who are hostile to him, for they are too numerous; the nobles on the other hand being but few, it becomes easy for a prince to make himself sure of them.

The worst that a prince may expect of a people who are unfriendly to him is that they will desert him; but the hostile nobles he has to fear, not only lest they abandon him, but also because they will turn against him. For they, being more far-sighted and astute, always save themselves in advance, and seek to secure the favour of him whom they hope may be successful. The prince also is obliged always to live with the same people; but he can do very well without the same nobles, whom he can make and unmake at will any day, and bestow upon them or deprive them of their rank whenever it pleases him. The better to elucidate this subject, we must consider the nobles mainly in two ways; that is to say, they either shape their conduct so as to ally themselves entirely to your fortunes, or they do not. Those who attach themselves to you thus, if they are not rapacious, are to be honoured and loved. Those who do not attach themselves to you must be regarded in two ways. Either they are influenced by pusillanimity and a natural lack of courage, and then you may make use of them, and especially of such as are men of intelligence; for in prosperity they will honour you, and in adversity you need not fear them. But if they purposely avoid attaching themselves to you from notions of ambition, then it is an evidence that they think more of their own interests than of yours; and of such men a prince must beware, and look upon them as open enemies, for when adversity comes they will always turn against him and contribute to his ruin.

Any one, therefore, who has become a prince by the favour of the people, must endeavour to preserve their good will, which will be easy for him, as they will ask of him no more than that he shall not oppress them. But he who, contrary to the will of the people, has become prince by the favour of the nobles, should at once and before everything else strive to win the good will of the people, which will be easy for him, by taking them under his protection. And as men, when they receive benefits from one of whom they expected only ill treatment, will attach themselves readily to such a benefactor, so the people will become more kindly disposed to such a one than if he had been made prince by their favour. Now a prince can secure the good will of the people in various ways, which differ with their character, and for which no fixed rules can be given. I will merely conclude by saying that it is essential for a prince to possess the good will and affection of his people, otherwise he will be utterly without support in time of adversity. Nabis, prince of Sparta, sustained the attacks of all Greece, and of a victorious Roman army, and successfully defended his country and his state against them; and when danger came, it was enough for him to be assured of a few supporters, which would not have sufficed if the people had been hostile to him. And let no one contravene this opinion of mine by quoting the trite saying, that 'he who relies upon the people builds upon quicksand'; though this may be true when a private citizen places his reliance upon the people in the belief that they will come to his relief when he is oppressed by his enemies or the magistrates. In such a case he will often find himself deceived; as happened in Rome to the Gracchi, and in Florence to Messer Scali. But it being a prince who places his reliance upon those whom he might command, and being a man of courage and undismayed by adversity, and not having neglected to make proper preparations, and keeping all animated by his own courageous example and by his orders, he will not be deceived by the people; and it will be seen that the foundations of his state are laid solidly.

Those princes run great risks who attempt to change a civil government into an absolute one; for such princes command either in person or by means of magistrates. In the latter case, their state is more feeble and precarious; for the prince is in all things dependent upon the will of those citizens who are placed at the head of the magistracy, who, particularly in times of adversity, may with great ease deprive him of the government, either by open opposition or by refusing him obedience. For when danger is upon him, the prince is no longer in time to assume absolute authority; for the citizens and subjects who have been accustomed to receive their commands from the magistrates will not be disposed to yield obedience to the prince when in adversity. Thus in doubtful times there will ever be a lack of men whom he can trust. Such a prince cannot depend upon what he observes in ordinary quiet times, when the citizens have need of his authority; for then everybody runs at his bidding, everybody promises, and everybody is willing to die for him, when death is very remote. But in adverse times, when the government has need of the citizens, then but few will be found to stand by the prince. And this experience is the more dangerous as it can only be made once.

A wise prince, therefore, will steadily pursue such a course that the citizens of his state will always and under all circumstances feel the need of his authority, and will therefore always prove faithful to him.

CHAPTER 10

In what manner the power of all principalities should be measured

In examining the nature of the different principalities, it is proper to consider another point; namely, whether a prince is sufficiently powerful to be able, in case of need, to sustain himself, or whether he is obliged always to depend upon others for his defence. And to explain this point the better, I say that, in my judgment, those are able to maintain themselves who, from an abundance of men and money, can put a well-appointed army into the field, and meet any one in open battle that may attempt to attack them. And I esteem those as having need of the constant support of others who cannot meet their enemies in the field, but are under the necessity of taking refuge behind walls and keeping within them. Of the first case I have already treated, and shall speak of it again hereafter as occasion may require. Of the second case I cannot say otherwise than that it behooves such princes to fortify the cities where they have their seat of government, and to provide them well with all necessary supplies, without paying much attention to the country. For any prince that has thoroughly fortified the city in which he resides, and has in other respects placed himself on a good footing with his subjects, as has been explained above, will not be readily attacked. For men will ever be indisposed to engage in enterprises that present manifest difficulties; and it cannot be regarded as an easy undertaking to attack a prince in a city which he has thoroughly fortified, and who is not hated by his people.

The cities of Germany enjoy great liberties; they own little land outside of the walls, and obey the emperor at their pleasure, fearing neither him nor any other neighbouring power; for they are so well fortified that their capture would manifestly be tedious and difficult. They all have suitable walls and ditches, and are amply supplied with artillery, and always keep in their public magazines a year's supply of provisions, drink, and fuel. Moreover, by way of feeding the people without expense to the public, they always keep on hand a common stock of raw materials to last for one year, so as to give employment in those branches of industry by which the people are accustomed to gain their living, and which are the nerve and life of the city. They also attach much importance to military exercises, and have established many regulations for their proper practice.

A prince, then, who has a well-fortified city, and has not made himself odious to his people, cannot be readily attacked; and if any one be nevertheless rash enough to make the attempt, he would have to abandon it ignominiously, for the things of this world are so uncertain that it seems almost impossible that any one should be able to remain a whole year with his army inactive, carrying on the siege.

And if any one were to argue that, if the people who have possessions outside of the city were to see them ravaged and destroyed by the enemy, they would lose their patience, and that their selfish desire to protect their property would cause them to forget their attachment to the prince, I would meet this objection by saying that a powerful and valiant prince will easily overcome this difficulty by encouraging his subjects with the hope that the evil will not endure long, or by alarming them with fears of the enemy's cruelty, or by assuring himself adroitly of those who have been too forward in expressing their discontent.

It is, moreover, reasonable to suppose that the enemy will ravage and destroy the country immediately upon his arrival before the city, and whilst its inhabitants are still full of courage and eager for defence. The prince, therefore, has the less ground for apprehension, because, by the time that the ardour of his people has cooled somewhat, the damage has already been done, and the evil is past remedy. And then the people will be the more ready to stand by their prince, for they will regard him as under obligations to them, their houses having been burnt and their property ravaged in his defence. For it is the nature of mankind to become as much attached to others by the benefits which they bestow on them, as by those which they receive.

All things considered, then, it will not be difficult for a prudent prince to keep up the courage of his citizens in time of siege, both in the beginning as well as afterwards, provided there be no lack of provisions or means of defence.

CHAPTER 11

Of ecclesiastical principalities

It remains now only to speak of ecclesiastical principalities, in the attainment of which all difficulties occur beforehand. To achieve them requires either virtue or good fortune; but they are maintained without either the one or the other, for they are sustained by the ancient ordinances of religion, which are so powerful and of such quality that they maintain their princes in their position, no matter what their conduct or mode of life may be. These are the only princes that have states without the necessity of defending them, and subjects without governing them; and their states, though undefended, are not taken from them, whilst their subjects are indifferent to the fact that they are not governed, and have no thought of the possibility of alienating themselves from their princes.

These ecclesiastical principalities, then, are the only ones that are secure and happy; and being under the direction of that supreme wisdom to which human minds cannot attain, I will abstain from all further discussion of them; for they are raised up and sustained by the Divine Power, and it would be a bold and presumptuous office for any man to discuss them.

Nevertheless, if any one asks how it comes that the Church has acquired such power and greatness in temporal matters, though previous to Alexander VI all the Italian potentates, and even the great barons and the smallest nobles, paid so little regard to the temporal power of the Church, whilst now a king of France trembles before it, and this power has been able to drive him out of Italy and to ruin the Venetians, I shall not deem it superfluous to recall to memory the circumstances of the growth of this temporal power, although they are well known.

Before King Charles VIII of France came into Italy, that country was under the rule of the Pope, the Venetians, the King of Naples, the Duke of Milan, and the Florentines. These powers were obliged always to keep in view two important points: the one, not to permit any foreign power to come into Italy with an armed force; and the other, to prevent each other from further aggrandisement.

Those who had to be most closely watched by the others were the Pope and the Venetians. To restrain the latter required the united power of all the others, as was the case in the defence of Ferrara; and to keep the Pope in check they availed themselves of the barons of Rome, who were divided into two factions, the Orsini and the Colonna; there being constant cause of quarrel between them, they were always with arms in hand, under the very eyes of the Pope, which kept the papal power weak and infirm.

And although now and then a courageous Pope arose, who succeeded for a time in repressing these factions, as for instance Sixtus IV, yet neither wisdom nor good fortune could ever relieve them entirely from this annoyance. The cause of this difficulty was the shortness of their lives; for in the ten years which is about the average length of the life of a Pope, it would be difficult for him to crush out either one of these factions entirely. And if, for instance, one Pope should have succeeded in putting down the Colonna, another one, hostile to the Orsini, would arise and resuscitate the Colonna, but would not have the time to put down the Orsini. This was the reason why the temporal power of the Popes was so little respected in Italy.

Afterwards Alexander VI came to the Pontificate, who, more than any of his predecessors, showed what a Pope could accomplish with the money and power of the Church. Availing himself of the opportunity of the French invasion of Italy, and the instrumentality of the Duke Valentino, Alexander accomplished all those things which I have mentioned when speaking of the actions of the duke. And although Alexander's object was not the aggrandisement of the Church, but rather that of his son, the duke, yet all his efforts served to advance the interests of the Church, which, after his death and that of his son, fell heir to all the results of his labours.

Soon after came Julius II, who found the Church powerful, and mistress of the entire Romagna, with the Roman barons crushed and the factions destroyed by the vigorous blows of Alexander. He also found the way prepared for the accumulation of money, which had never been employed before the time of Alexander. Julius II not only continued the system of Alexander, but carried it even further, and resolved to acquire the possession of Bologna, to ruin the Venetians, and to drive the French out of Italy, in all of which he succeeded. And this was the more praiseworthy in him, inasmuch as he did all these things, not for his own aggrandisement, but for that of the Church. He furthermore restrained the Orsini and the Colonna factions within the limits in which he found them upon his accession to the Pontificate; and although there were some attempts at disturbances between them, yet there were two things that kept them down: one, the power of the Church, which overawed them; and the other, the fact that neither of them had any cardinals, who were generally the fomenters of the disturbances between them. Nor will these party feuds ever cease so long as the cardinals take any part in them. For it is they who stir up the factions in Rome as well as elsewhere, and then force the barons to sustain them. And it is thus that the ambition of these prelates gives rise to the discord and the disturbances amongst the barons.

His Holiness Pope Leo X thus found the Church all-powerful on his accession; and it is to be hoped that, if his predecessors have made the Church great by means of arms, he will make her still greater and more venerable by his goodness and his infinite other virtues.

CHAPTER 12

Of the different kinds of troops,
and of mercenaries

Having discussed in detail the characteristics of all those kinds of principalities of which I proposed at the outset to treat, and having examined to some extent the causes of their success or failure, and explained the means by which many have sought to acquire and maintain them, it remains for me now to discuss generally the means of offence and defence which such princes may have to employ, under the various circumstances above referred to.

We have said how necessary it is for a prince to lay solid foundations for his power, as without such he would inevitably be ruined. The main foundations which all states must have, whether new, or old, or mixed, are good laws and good armies. And as there can be no good laws where there are not good armies, so the laws will be apt to be good where the armies are so. I will therefore leave the question of the laws, and confine myself to that of the armies. I say, then, that the armies with which a prince defends his state are either his own, or they are mercenaries or auxiliaries, or they are mixed. Mercenary and auxiliary troops are both useless and dangerous; and if any one attempts to found his state upon mercenaries, it will never be stable or secure; for they are disunited, ambitious and without discipline – faithless and braggarts amongst friends, but amongst enemies cowards, and have neither fear of God nor good faith with men; so that the ruin of the prince who depends on them will be deferred only just so long as attack is delayed; in peace he will be spoliated by his mercenaries, and in war by his enemies. The reason of all this is, that mercenary troops are not influenced by affection, or by any other consideration except their small stipend, which is not enough to make them willing to die for you. They are ready to serve you as soldiers so long as you are at peace; but when war comes, they will either run away or march off. There is no difficulty in demonstrating the truth of this; for the present ruin of Italy can be attributed to nothing else but the fact that she has for many years depended upon mercenary armies, who for a time had some success, and seemed brave enough amongst themselves, but so soon as a foreign enemy came they showed what stuff they were made of. This was the reason why Charles VIII, King of France, was allowed to take Italy with scarcely an effort, and as it were with merely a piece of chalk. [Charles VIII had merely to send a quartermaster ahead with 'a piece of chalk' to mark the houses in which the French troops were to be quartered.] Those who assert that our misfortunes were caused by our own faults speak the truth; but these faults were not such as are generally supposed to have been the cause, but those rather which I have pointed out; and as it was the princes who committed these faults, so they also suffered the penalties.

I will demonstrate more fully the unhappy consequences of employing mercenary armies. Their commanders are either competent, or they are not; if they are, then you cannot trust them, because their chief aim will always be their own aggrandisement, either by imposing upon you, who are their employer, or by oppressing others beyond your intentions; and if they are incompetent, then they will certainly hasten your ruin. If now you meet these remarks by saying that the same will be the case with every commander, whether of mercenary troops or others, I reply that inasmuch as armies are employed either by princes or by republics, the prince should always in person perform the duty of commanding his army, and a republic should send one of her own citizens to command her troops, and in case he should not be successful, then they must change him; but if he is victorious, then they must be careful to keep him within the law, so that he may not exceed his powers. Experience has shown that princes as well as republics achieve the greatest success in war when they themselves direct the movements of their own armies, whilst mercenary troops do nothing but damage; and that a republic that has armies of her own is much less easily subjected to servitude by one of her own citizens, than one that depends upon foreign troops.

Thus Rome and Sparta maintained their liberties for many centuries by having armies of their own; the Swiss are most thoroughly armed, and consequently enjoy the greatest independence and liberty. The Carthaginians, on the other hand, furnish an example of the danger of employing mercenaries, for they came very near being subjugated by them at the close of the first war with Rome, although they had appointed some of their own citizens as commanders. After the death of Epaminondas, the Thebans made Philip of Macedon commander of their army, who after having been victorious deprived the Thebans of their liberty. The Milanese, after the death of Duke Philip, employed Francesco Sforza against the Venetians; after having defeated them at Caravaggio, he combined with them to subjugate his employers, the Milanese. The father of Francesco Sforza, who was commander in the service of Queen Joanna of Naples, suddenly left her entirely without troops, in consequence of which she was compelled to throw herself upon the protection of the King of Aragon, to save her kingdom. And if the Venetians and the Florentines formerly extended their dominions by means of mercenaries, and without their commanders attempting to make themselves princes of the country, but rather defending it loyally, I can only say that the Florentines were greatly favoured by fortune in that respect. For of the valiant captains whose ambition they might have feared, some were not victorious, some never met an enemy, and others directed their ambition elsewhere. Amongst those who were not victorious was Giovanni Aguto [John Sharpe], whose good faith was never put to the test, he having been unsuccessful in the field; although it will be generally admitted that, had he been successful, the Florentines would have been at his mercy. The Sforzas and the Bracceschi were always opposed to each other, which caused Francesco to direct his ambition towards Lombardy, whilst Braccio turned his towards the Church and the kingdom of Naples.

But let us come now to occurrences of more recent date. The Florentines had conferred the command of their troops upon Paolo Vitelli, a soldier of the greatest ability, who had risen from private station to the highest post and reputation. No one will deny that, if he had succeeded in taking Pisa, the Florentines would have been obliged to submit to him; for had he gone over to the enemy, they would have been helpless, and if they kept him they would have been obliged to submit to his terms.

If now we look at the Venetians, we shall find that they carried on their wars securely and gloriously so long as they confined themselves to their proper element, the water, where they conducted their operations most bravely with their nobles and their own people. But when they engaged in wars on land, they no longer acted with their customary bravery, and adopted the habit of the other Italian states of employing mercenary troops. And although at the beginning of the growth of their dominion on land they had no occasion to have any serious apprehensions of their commanders, because their own reputation was great and their possessions on land small, yet when they extended these, which was under the captaincy of Carmignuola, they became sensible of their error. For although they were aware that it was by his superior conduct that they had defeated the Duke of Milan, yet on observing his lukewarmness in the further conduct of the war, they concluded that they could no longer hope for victory under his command. Still they dared not dismiss him for fear of losing what they had gained, and therefore they deemed it necessary for their own security to put him to death.

After that, the Venetians employed as generals of their forces Bartolomeo da Bergamo, Roberto da San Severino, the Count Pitigliano and the like, with whom they had reason rather to apprehend losses than to expect successes; as indeed happened afterwards at Vaila, where in one battle they lost what had taken them eight hundred years of great labour to acquire; for with this kind of troops acquisitions are feeble and slow, whilst losses are quick and extraordinary.

Having thus far confined my examples to Italy, which has been for many years controlled by mercenary armies, I will now go back to an earlier period in discussing this subject; so that, having seen the origin and progress of the system, it may be the more effectually corrected. You must know, then, that in the earlier times, so soon as the Roman Empire began to lose its power and credit in Italy, and when the Pope acquired more influence in temporal matters, Italy became subdivided into a number of states. Many of the large cities took up arms against their nobles, who, encouraged by the emperor, had kept them oppressed. The

Church, by way of increasing her own influence in temporal matters, favoured this revolt of the cities against their nobles. In many other cities the supreme power was usurped by some of their own citizens, who made themselves princes of the same. Thus it was that Italy, as it were, passed under the dominion of the Church and certain republics. And as these citizens and prelates were not accustomed to the management of armies, they began to hire foreigners for this purpose. The first who brought this sort of military into high repute was Alberigo da Como, a native of the Romagna. It was under his discipline that Braccio and Sforza were trained, and these in turn became the arbiters of Italy. They were succeeded by all those others who up to our time have led the armies of Italy; and the result of all their valour was that she was overrun by the French under Charles VIII, ravaged and plundered by Louis XII, oppressed by Ferdinand of Spain, and insulted and vituperated by the Swiss.

The course which these mercenary leaders pursued for the purpose of giving reputation and credit to their own mounted forces was, first, to decry and destroy the reputation of the infantry of the several states. They did this because, having no territorial possessions of their own, and being mere soldiers of fortune, they could achieve no reputation by means of a small body of infantry, and for a larger force they could not furnish subsistence. And therefore they confined themselves to cavalry, a smaller force of which enabled them the more readily to gain success and credit, and was at the same time more easily subsisted. In this way they brought matters to that point, that in an army of twenty thousand there were not over two thousand infantry.

Moreover, they used all means and ingenuity to avoid exposing themselves and their men to great fatigue and danger, and never killing each other in their encounters, but merely taking prisoners, who were afterwards liberated without ransom. They never made any night attacks when besieging a place, nor did the besieged make any night sorties; they never properly entrenched their camps, and never kept the field in winter. All these practices were permitted by their rules of war, which were devised by them expressly, as we have said, to avoid hardships and danger; so that Italy was brought to shame and slavery by this system of employing mercenary troops.

CHAPTER 13

Of auxiliaries, and of mixed and national troops

Auxiliary troops, which are the other kind which I have characterised in the preceding chapter as useless, are such as are furnished by a powerful ally whom a prince calls upon to come with his troops to aid and defend him; as was done quite lately by Pope Julius II, who, having had sad proof of the inefficiency of mercenaries in his attempt upon Ferrara, resorted to auxiliaries, and arranged with Ferdinand of Spain to send his armies to his assistance.

Troops of this kind may be useful and good in themselves, but they are always dangerous for him who calls them to his aid; for if defeated, he remains undone, and if victorious, then he is in their power like a prisoner. And although I could adduce numerous examples of this from ancient history, yet I will here cite that of Pope Julius II, which is still fresh in our minds, and whose conduct in that respect could not well have been more imprudent than what it was. For, wishing to take Ferrara, he placed himself entirely in the hands of a foreigner. Fortunately for him, however, an incident occurred which saved him from the full effect of his bad selection; for his auxiliaries having been defeated at Ravenna, the Swiss suddenly appeared on the field and put the victors to ignominious flight. And thus Julius II escaped becoming prisoner either to his enemies who had fled, or to his auxiliaries; for the enemy's defeat was not due to their assistance, but to that of others.

The Florentines, having no army of their own, and wishing to get possession of Pisa, employed for that purpose ten thousand French troops, and were involved in greater danger by them than they had ever experienced from any other difficulty. The Emperor of Constantinople, by way of resisting the attacks of his neighbours, put ten thousand troops into Greece, who at the termination of the war refused to leave the country again; and this was the beginning of the subjection of Greece to the infidels.

Whoever, then, desires not to be victorious, let him employ auxiliary troops, for they are much more dangerous even than mercenaries. For your ruin is certain with auxiliaries, who are all united in their obedience to another; whilst mercenaries, even after victory, need more time and greater opportunity to injure you, for they are not one homogeneous body, and have been selected by yourself and are in your pay, and their commander being appointed by you, he cannot so quickly gain sufficient influence over these troops to enable him to injure you. In short, with mercenaries the danger lies in their cowardice and bad faith; whilst with auxiliaries their valour constitutes the danger.

A wise prince, therefore, should ever avoid employing either one of them, and should rely exclusively upon his own troops, and should prefer defeat with them rather than victory with the troops of others, with whom no real victory can ever be won. In proof of this, I shall not hesitate again to cite the conduct of Cesare Borgia. This duke entered the Romagna with auxiliaries, taking there only French troops, with whom he took Imola and Fourli. But thinking afterwards that these troops were not reliable, he had recourse to mercenaries, whom he deemed less dangerous, and engaged the Orsini and the Vitelli. These, however, proved themselves by their conduct to be uncertain, faithless, and dangerous; and therefore the duke destroyed them, and then relied upon his own troops exclusively. The difference between the one and the other of these troops is easily seen when we look at the reputation of the Duke Valentino at the time when he employed the Orsini and the Vitelli, and when he had none but his own troops; for then his credit increased steadily, and the duke was never more highly esteemed than when every one saw that he was thoroughly master of his armies.

I did not intend to depart from Italian and recent instances, and yet I cannot leave unnoticed the case of Hiero of Syracuse, being one of those to whom I have referred before. Having been made general of the Syracusan army, as before stated, he quickly perceived that mercenary troops were not useful, their commanders being appointed in a similar manner as our Italian condottieri. And as it seemed to Hiero that he could neither keep nor dismiss them with safety, he had them all put to death and cut to pieces, and thenceforth carried on the war exclusively with troops of his own.

I will also recall to memory an illustration from the Old Testament applicable to this subject. David having offered to go and fight the Philistine bully, Goliath, Saul, by way of encouraging David, gave him his own arms and armour, which David however declined, after having tried them, saying that he could not make the most of his strength if he used those arms; and therefore he preferred to meet the enemy with no other arms but his sling and his knife. In short, the armour of another never suits you entirely; it is either too large and falls off your back, or weighs you down, or it is too tight.

Charles VII, father of Louis XI, King of France, having by his valour and good fortune delivered France from the English, recognised the necessity of depending solely upon his own armies, and organised in his kingdom regular companies of artillery, cavalry and infantry. His son, Louis XI, afterwards disbanded the infantry, and began to hire Swiss soldiers in their stead. This error, being followed by others, is now seen to have been the cause of the dangers to which that kingdom was exposed; for by giving prominence to the Swiss, Louis depreciated his own troops, and having disbanded his own infantry entirely, and accustomed his mounted forces to the support of the Swiss, they felt that they could have no success without them. Thence it came that the French could not hold their own against the Swiss, and without their support they could not stand against others. And thus the French armies have remained mixed, that is to say, partly their own troops and partly mercenaries; which, although better than either auxiliaries or mercenaries alone, yet makes them much worse than if they were composed exclusively of their own troops. Let this example suffice; for the kingdom of France would have been invincible if the military system established by Charles VII had been persevered in and extended. But the short-sightedness of men leads them to adopt any measure that for the moment seems good, and which does not openly reveal the poison concealed under it, as I have said above of hectic fevers.

A prince, then, who does not promptly recognise evils as they arise, cannot be called wise; but unfortunately this faculty is given to but few. And if we reflect upon the beginning of the ruin of the Roman Empire, it will be found to have resulted solely from hiring the Goths for its armies; for that was the first cause of the enervation of the forces of the empire; and the valour of which the Romans divested themselves was thus transferred to the Goths.

I conclude, then, that no prince can ever be secure that has not an army of his own; and he will become wholly dependent upon fortune if in times of adversity he lacks the valour to defend himself. And wise men have ever held the opinion, that nothing is more weak and unstable than the reputation of power when not founded upon forces of the prince's own; by which I mean armies composed of his own subjects or citizens, or of his own creation; all others are either mercenaries or auxiliaries.

The means for organising such armies of his own will readily be found by the prince by studying the method in which Philip of Macedon, father of Alexander the Great, and many republics and princes, organised their armies, to which I refer in all respects.

CHAPTER 14

Of the duties of a prince in relation to military matters

A prince, then, should have no other thought or object so much at heart, and make no other thing so much his especial study, as the art of war and the organisation and discipline of his army; for that is the only art that is expected of him who commands. And such is its power, that it not only maintains in their position those who were born princes, but it often enables men born in private station to achieve the rank of princes. And on the other hand, we have seen that princes who thought more of indulgence in pleasure than of arms have thereby lost their states.

Thus the neglect of the art of war is the principal cause of the loss of your state, whilst a proficiency in it often enables you to acquire one. Francesco Sforza, from being skilled in arms, rose from private station to be Duke of Milan; and his descendants, by shunning the labours and fatigue of arms, relapsed into the condition of private citizens.

Amongst the other causes of evil that will befall a prince who is destitute of a proper military force is, that it will make him contemned; which is one of those disgraces against which a prince ought especially to guard, as we shall demonstrate further on. For there is no sort of proportion between one who is well armed and one who is not so; nor is it reasonable that he who is armed should voluntarily obey the unarmed, or that a prince who is without a military force should remain secure amongst his armed subjects. For when there is disdain on the one side and mistrust on the other, it is impossible that the two should work well together. A prince, then, who is not master of the art of war, besides other misfortunes, cannot be respected by his soldiers, nor can he depend upon them. And therefore should the practice of arms ever be uppermost in the prince's thoughts; he should study it in time of peace as much as in actual war, which he can do in two ways, the one by practical exercise, and the other by scientific study. As regards the former, he must not only keep his troops well disciplined and exercised, but he must also frequently follow the chase, whereby his body will become inured to hardships, and he will become familiar with the character of the country, and learn where the mountains rise and the valleys debouch, and how the plains lie; he will learn to know the nature of rivers and of the swamps, to all of which he should give the greatest attention. For this knowledge is valuable in many ways to the prince, who thereby learns to know his own country, and can therefore better understand its defence. Again, by the knowledge of and practical acquaintance with one country, he will with greater facility comprehend the character of others, which it may be necessary for him to understand. For instance, the mountains, valleys, plains, rivers and swamps of Tuscany bear a certain resemblance to those of other provinces, so that by the knowledge of the character and formation of one country he will readily arrive at that of others. A prince who is wanting in that experience lacks the very first essentials which a commander should possess; for that knowledge teaches him where to find the enemy, to select proper places for entrenchments, to conduct armies, regulate marches and order battles, and to keep the field with advantage.

Amongst other praises that have been accorded by different writers to Philopoemen, prince of the Achaeans, was that in time of peace he devoted himself constantly to the study of the art of war; and when he walked in the country with friends, he often stopped and argued with them thus: 'Suppose the enemy were on yonder mountain, and we should happen to be here with our army, which of the two would have the advantage? How could we go most safely to find the enemy, observing proper order? If we should wish to retreat, how should we proceed? And if the enemy were to retreat, which way had we best pursue him?' And thus in walking he proposed to his friends all the cases that possibly could occur with an army, hearing their opinions, and giving his own, and corroborating them with reasons; so that by these continued discussions no case could ever arise in the conduct of an army for which he had not thought of the proper remedy. As regards the exercise of the mind, the prince should read history, and therein study the actions of eminent men, observe how they bore themselves in war, and examine the causes of their victories and defeats, so that he may imitate the former and avoid the latter. But above all should he follow the example of whatever distinguished man he may have chosen for his model; assuming that some one has been specially praised and held up to him as glorious, whose actions and exploits he should ever bear in mind. Thus it is told of Alexander that he imitated Achilles, and of Caesar that he had taken Alexander for his model as Scipio had done with Cyrus. And whoever reads the life of Cyrus, written by Xenophon, will not fail to recognise afterwards, in the life of Scipio, of how much value this imitation was to him, and how closely the latter conformed in point of temperance, affability, humanity and liberality to the accounts given of Cyrus by Xenophon.

A wise prince, then, should act in like manner and should never be idle in times of peace, but should industriously lay up stores of which to avail himself in times of adversity; so that, when Fortune abandons him, he may be prepared to resist her blows.

CHAPTER 15

Of the means by which men, and especially princes, win applause or incur censure

It remains now to be seen in what manner a prince should conduct himself towards his subjects and his allies; and knowing that this matter has already been treated by many others, I apprehend that my writing upon it also may be deemed presumptuous, especially as in the discussion of the same I shall differ from the rules laid down by others. But as my aim is to write something that may be useful to him for whom it is intended, it seems to me proper to pursue the real truth of the matter, rather than to indulge in mere speculation on the same; for many have imagined republics and principalities such as have never been known to exist in reality. For the manner in which men live is so different from the way in which they ought to live, that he who leaves the common course for that which he ought to follow will find that it leads him to ruin rather than to safety. For a man who, in all respects, will carry out only his professions of good, will be apt to be ruined amongst so many who are evil. A prince therefore who desires to maintain himself must learn to be not always good, but to be so or not as necessity may require. Leaving aside then the imaginary things concerning princes, and confining ourselves only to the realities, I say that all men when they are spoken of, and more especially princes, from being in a more conspicuous position, are noted for some quality that brings them either praise or censure. Thus one is deemed liberal, another miserly (*misero*), to use a Tuscan expression (for avaricious is he who by rapine desires to gain, and miserly we call him who abstains too much from the enjoyment of his own). One man is esteemed generous, another rapacious; one cruel, another merciful; one faithless, and another faithful; one effeminate and pusillanimous, another ferocious and brave; one affable, another haughty; one lascivious, another chaste; one sincere, the other cunning; one facile, another inflexible; one grave, another frivolous; one religious, another sceptical; and so on.

I am well aware that it would be most praiseworthy for a prince to possess all of the above-named qualities that are esteemed good; but as he cannot have them all, nor entirely observe them, because of his human nature which does not permit it, he should at least be prudent enough to know how to avoid the infamy of those vices that would rob him of his state; and if possible also to guard against such as are likely to endanger it. But if that be not possible, then he may with less hesitation follow his natural inclinations. Nor need he care about incurring censure for such vices, without which the preservation of his state may be difficult. For, all things considered, it will be found that some things that seem like virtue will lead you to ruin if you follow them; whilst others, that apparently are vices, will, if followed, result in your safety and well-being.

CHAPTER 16

Of liberality and parsimoniousness

To begin with the first of the above-named qualities, I say that it is well for a prince to be deemed liberal; and yet liberality, indulged in so that you will no longer be feared, will prove injurious. For liberality worthily exercised, as it should be, will not be recognised, and may bring upon you the reproach of the very opposite. For if you desire the reputation of being liberal, you must not stop at any degree of sumptuousness; so that a prince will in this way generally consume his entire substance, and may in the end, if he wishes to keep up his reputation for liberality, be obliged to subject his people to extraordinary burdens, and resort to taxation, and employ all sorts of measures that will enable him to procure money. This will soon make him odious with his people; and when he becomes poor, he will be contemned by everybody; so that having by his prodigality injured many and benefited few, he will be the first to suffer every inconvenience, and be exposed to every danger. And when he becomes conscious of this and attempts to retrench, he will at once expose himself to the imputation of being a miser.

A prince then, being unable without injury to himself to practise the virtue of liberality in such manner that it may be generally recognised, should not, when he becomes aware of this and is prudent, mind incurring the charge of parsimoniousness. For after a while, when it is seen that by his prudence and economy he makes his revenues suffice him, and that he is able to provide for his defence in case of war, and engage in enterprises without burdening his people, he will be considered liberal enough by all those from whom he takes nothing, and these are the many; whilst only those to whom he does not give, and which are the few, will look upon him as parsimonious.

In our own times we have not seen any great things accomplished except by those who were regarded as parsimonious; all others have been ruined. Pope Julius II, having been helped by his reputation of liberality to attain the Pontificate, did not afterwards care to keep up that reputation to enable him to engage in war against the King of France; and he carried on ever so many wars without levying any extraordinary taxes. For his long-continued economy enabled him to supply the extraordinary expenses of his wars.

If the present King of Spain had sought the reputation of being liberal he would not have been able to engage in so many enterprises, nor could he have carried them to a successful issue. A prince, then, who would avoid robbing his own subjects, and be able to defend himself, and who would avoid becoming poor and abject or rapacious, should not mind incurring the reputation of being parsimonious; for that is one of those vices that will enable him to maintain his state. And should it be alleged that Julius Caesar attained the empire by means of his liberality, and that many others by the same reputation have achieved the highest rank, then I reply, that you are either already a prince, or are in the way of becoming one; in the first case liberality would be injurious to you, but in the second it certainly is necessary to be reputed liberal. Now Caesar was aiming to attain the empire of Rome; but having achieved it, had he lived and not moderated his expenditures, he would assuredly have ruined the empire by his prodigality.

And were any one to assert that there have been many princes who have achieved great things with their armies, and who were accounted most liberal, I answer that a prince either spends his own substance and that of his subjects, or that of others. Of the first two he should be very sparing, but in spending that of others he ought not to omit any act of liberality. The prince who in person leads his armies into foreign countries, and supports them by plunder, pillage and exactions, and thus dispenses the substance of others, should do so with the greatest liberality, as otherwise his soldiers would not follow him. For that which belongs neither to him nor to his own subjects, a prince may spend most lavishly, as was done by Cyrus, Caesar and Alexander. The spending of other people's substance will not diminish, but rather increase, his reputation; it is only the spending of his own that is injurious to a prince.

And there is nothing that consumes itself so quickly as liberality; for the very act of using it causes it to lose the faculty of being used, and will either impoverish and make you contemned, or it will make you rapacious and odious. And of all the things against which a prince should guard most carefully is the incurring the hatred and contempt of his subjects. Now, liberality will bring upon you either the one or the other; there is therefore more wisdom in submitting to be called parsimonious, which may bring you blame without hatred, than, by aiming to be called liberal, to incur unavoidably the reputation of rapacity, which will bring upon you infamy as well as hatred.

CHAPTER 17

Of cruelty and clemency, and whether it is better to be loved than feared

Coming down now to the other aforementioned qualities, I say that every prince ought to desire the reputation of being merciful, and not cruel; at the same time, he should be careful not to misuse that mercy. Cesare Borgia was reputed cruel, yet by his cruelty he reunited the Romagna to his states, and restored that province to order, peace and loyalty; and if we carefully examine his course, we shall find it to have been really much more merciful than the course of the people of Florence, who, to escape the reputation of cruelty, allowed Pistoia to be destroyed. A prince, therefore, should not mind the ill repute of cruelty, when he can thereby keep his subjects united and loyal; for a few displays of severity will really be more merciful than to allow, by an excess of clemency, disorders to occur, which are apt to result in rapine and murder; for these injure a whole community, whilst the executions ordered by the prince fall only upon a few individuals. And, above all others, the new prince will find it almost impossible to avoid the reputation of cruelty, because new states are generally exposed to many dangers. It was on this account that Virgil made Dido to excuse the severity of her government, because it was still new, saying –

> Res dura, et regni novitas me talia cogunt
> Moliri, et late fines custode tueri.
>
> [My cruel fate,
> And doubts attending an unsettled state,
> Force me to guard my coasts from foreign foes.
> DRYDEN]

A prince, however, should be slow to believe and to act; nor should he be too easily alarmed by his own fears, and should proceed moderately and with prudence and humanity, so that an excess of confidence may not make him incautious, nor too much mistrust make him intolerant. This, then, gives rise to the question 'whether it be better to be beloved than feared, or to be feared than beloved'. It will naturally be answered that it would be desirable to be both the one and the other; but as it is difficult to be both at the same time, it is much more safe to be feared than to be loved, when you have to choose between the two. For it may be said of men in general that they are ungrateful and fickle, dissemblers, avoiders of danger, and greedy of gain. So long as you shower benefits upon them, they are all yours; they offer you their blood, their substance, their lives and their children, provided the necessity for it is far off; but when it is near at hand, then they revolt. And the prince who relies upon their words, without having otherwise provided for his security, is ruined; for friendships that are by rewards, and not by greatness and nobility of soul, although deserved, yet are not real, and cannot be depended upon in time of adversity.

Besides, men have less hesitation in offending one who makes himself beloved than one who makes himself feared; for love holds by a bond of obligation which, as mankind is bad, is broken on every occasion whenever it is for the interest of the obliged party to break it. But fear holds by the apprehension of punishment, which never leaves men. A prince, however, should make himself feared in such a manner that, if he has not won the affections of his people, he shall at least not incur their hatred; for the being feared, and not hated, can go very well together, if the prince abstains from taking the substance of his subjects, and leaves them their women. And if you should be obliged to inflict capital punishment upon any one, then be sure to do so only when there is manifest cause and proper justification for it; and, above all things, abstain from taking people's property, for men will sooner forget the death of their fathers than the loss of their patrimony. Besides, there will never be any lack of reasons for taking people's property; and a prince who once begins to live by rapine will ever find excuses for seizing other people's property. On the other hand, reasons for taking life are not so easily found, and are more readily exhausted. But when a prince is at the head of his army, with a multitude of soldiers under his command, then it is above all things necessary for him to disregard the reputation of cruelty; for without such severity an army cannot be kept together, nor disposed for any successful feat of arms.

Amongst the many admirable qualities of Hannibal, it is related of him that, having an immense army composed of a very great variety of races of men, which he led to war in foreign countries, no quarrels ever occurred amongst them, nor were there ever any dissensions between them and their chief, either in his good or in his adverse fortunes; which can only be accounted for by his extreme cruelty. This, together with his boundless courage, made him ever venerated and terrible in the eyes of his soldiers; and without that extreme severity all his other virtues would not have sufficed to produce that result.

Inconsiderate writers have, on the one hand, admired his great deeds, and, on the other, condemned the principal cause of the same. And the proof that his other virtues would not have sufficed him may be seen from the case of Scipio, who was one of the most remarkable men, not only of his own time, but in all history. His armies revolted in Spain solely in consequence of his extreme clemency, which allowed his soldiers more licence than comports with proper military discipline. This fact was censured in the Roman senate by Fabius Maximus, who called Scipio the corrupter of the Roman soldiers. The tribe of the Locrians having been wantonly destroyed by one of the lieutenants of Scipio, he neither punished him for that nor for his insolence – simply because of his own easy nature; so that, when somebody wished to excuse Scipio in the senate, he said 'that there were many men who knew better how to avoid errors themselves than to punish them in others'. This easy nature of Scipio's would in time have dimmed his fame and glory if he had persevered in it under the empire; but living as he did under the government of the senate, this dangerous quality of his was not only covered up, but actually redounded to his honour.

To come back now to the question whether it be better to be beloved than feared, I conclude that, as men love of their own free will, but are inspired with fear by the will of the prince, a wise prince should always rely upon himself, and not upon the will of others, but above all should he always strive to avoid being hated, as I have already said above.

CHAPTER 18

In what manner princes should keep their faith

It must be evident to every one that it is more praiseworthy for a prince always to maintain good faith, and practise integrity rather than craft and deceit. And yet the experience of our own times has shown that those princes have achieved great things who made small account of good faith, and who understood by cunning to circumvent the intelligence of others; and that in the end they got the better of those whose actions were dictated by loyalty and good faith. You must know, therefore, that there are two ways of carrying on a contest; the one by law, and the other by force. The first is practised by men, and the other by animals; and as the first is often insufficient, it becomes necessary to resort to the second.

A prince then should know how to employ the nature of man, and that of the beasts as well. This was figuratively taught by ancient writers, who relate how Achilles and many other princes were given to Chiron the centaur to be nurtured, and how they were trained under his tutorship; which fable means nothing else than that their preceptor combined the qualities of the man and the beast; and that a prince, to succeed, will have to employ both the one and the other nature, as the one without the other cannot produce lasting results.

It being necessary then for a prince to know well how to employ the nature of the beasts, he should be able to assume both that of the fox and that of the lion; for whilst the latter cannot escape the traps laid for him, the former cannot defend himself against the wolves. A prince should be a fox, to know the traps and snares; and a lion, to be able to frighten the wolves; for those who simply hold to the nature of the lion do not understand their business.

A sagacious prince then cannot and should not fulfil his pledges when their observance is contrary to his interest, and when the causes that induced him to pledge his faith no longer exist. If men were all good, then indeed this precept would be bad; but as men are naturally bad, and will not observe their faith towards you, you must, in the same way, not observe yours to them; and no prince ever yet lacked legitimate reasons with which to colour his want of good faith. Innumerable modern examples could be given of this; and it could easily be shown how many treaties of peace, and how many engagements, have been made null and void by the faithlessness of princes; and he who has best known how to play the fox has ever been the most successful.

But it is necessary that the prince should know how to colour this nature well, and how to be a great hypocrite and dissembler. For men are so simple, and yield so much to immediate necessity, that the deceiver will never lack dupes. I will mention one of the most recent examples. Alexander VI never did nor ever thought of anything but to deceive, and always found a reason for doing so. No one ever had greater skill in asseverating, or who affirmed his pledges with greater oaths and observed them less, than Pope Alexander; and yet he was always successful in his deceits, because he knew the weakness of men in that particular.

It is not necessary, however, for a prince to possess all the above-mentioned qualities; but it is essential that he should at least seem to have them. I will even venture to say, that to have and to practise them constantly is pernicious, but to seem to have them is useful. For instance, a prince should seem to be merciful, faithful, humane, religious and upright, and should even be so in reality; but he should have his mind so trained that, when occasion requires it, he may know how to change to the opposite. And it must be understood that a prince, and especially one who has but recently acquired his state, cannot perform all those things which cause men to be esteemed as good; he being often obliged, for the sake of maintaining his state, to act contrary to humanity, charity and religion. And therefore is it necessary that he should have a versatile mind, capable of changing readily, according as the winds and changes of fortune bid him; and, as has been said above, not to swerve from the good if possible, but to know how to resort to evil if necessity demands it.

A prince then should be very careful never to allow anything to escape his lips that does not abound in the above-named five qualities, so that to see and to hear him he may seem all charity, integrity and humanity, all uprightness and all piety. And more than all else is it necessary for a prince to seem to possess the last quality; for mankind in general judge more by what they see and hear than by what they feel, every one being capable of the former, and but few of the latter. Everybody sees what you seem to be, but few really feel what you are; and these few dare not oppose the opinion of the many, who are protected by the majesty of the state; for the actions of all men, and especially those of princes, are judged by the result, where there is no other judge to whom to appeal.

A prince then should look mainly to the successful maintenance of his state. The means which he employs for this will always be accounted honourable, and will be praised by everybody; for the common people are always taken by appearances and by results, and it is the vulgar mass that constitutes the world. But a very few have rank and station, whilst the many have nothing to sustain them. A certain prince of our time [Ferdinand of Aragon], whom it is well not to name, never preached anything but peace and good faith; but if he had always observed either the one or the other, it would in most instances have cost him his reputation or his state.

CHAPTER 19

A prince must avoid being contemned and hated

Having thus considered separately the most important of the above-mentioned qualities which a prince should possess, I will now briefly discuss the others under this general maxim: that a prince should endeavour, as has already been said, to avoid everything that would tend to make him odious and contemned. And in proportion as he avoids that will he have performed his part well, and need fear no danger from any other vices. Above all, a prince makes himself odious by rapacity, that is, by taking away from his subjects their property and their women, from which he should carefully abstain. The great mass of men will live quietly and contentedly, provided you do not rob them of their substance and their honour; so that you will have to contend only with the ambition of a few, which is easily restrained in various ways.

A prince becomes despised when he incurs by his acts the reputation of being variable, inconstant, effeminate, pusillanimous, and irresolute; he should therefore guard against this as against a dangerous rock, and should strive to display in all his actions grandeur, courage, gravity and determination. And in judging the private causes of his subjects, his decisions should be irrevocable. Thus will he maintain himself in such esteem that no one will think of deceiving or betraying him. The prince, who by his habitual conduct gives cause for such an opinion of himself, will acquire so great a reputation that it will be difficult to conspire against him, or to attack him; provided that it be generally known that he is truly excellent, and revered by his subjects. For there are two things which a prince has to fear: the one, attempts against him by his own subjects; and the other, attacks from without by powerful foreigners. Against the latter he will be able to defend himself by good armies and good allies, and whoever has the one will not lack the other. And so long as his external affairs are kept quiet, his internal security will not be disturbed, unless it should be by a conspiracy. And even if he were to be assailed from without, if he has a well-organised army and has lived as he should have done, he will always (unless he should give way himself) be able to withstand any such attacks, as we have related was done by Nabis, tyrant of Sparta. But even when at peace externally, it nevertheless behooves the prince to be on his guard, lest his subjects conspire against him secretly. He will, however, be sufficiently secure against this, if he avoids being hated and despised, and keeps his subjects well satisfied with himself, which should ever be his aim, as I have already explained above. Not to be hated nor contemned by the mass of the people is one of the best safeguards for a prince against conspiracies; for conspirators always believe that the death of the prince will be satisfactory to the people; but when they know that it will rather offend than conciliate the people, they will not venture upon such a course, for the difficulties that surround conspirators are infinite.

Experience proves that, although there have been many conspiracies, yet but few have come to a good end; for he who conspires cannot act alone, nor can he take any associates except such as he believes to be malcontents; and so soon as you divulge your plans to a malcontent, you furnish him the means wherewith to procure satisfaction. For by denouncing it he may hope to derive great advantages for himself, seeing that such a course will insure him those advantages, whilst the other is full of doubts and dangers. He must indeed be a very rare friend of yours, or an inveterate enemy of the prince, to observe good faith and not to betray you.

But to reduce this matter to a few words, I say that on the side of the conspirator there is nothing but fear, jealousy and apprehension of punishment; whilst the prince has on his side the majesty of sovereignty, the laws, the support of his friends and of the government, which protect him. And if to all this be added the popular good will, it seems impossible that any one should be rash enough to attempt a conspiracy against him. For ordinarily a conspirator has cause for apprehension only before the execution of his evil purpose; but in this case, having the people for his enemies, he has also to fear the consequences after the commission of the crime, and can look nowhere for a refuge. Upon this point I might adduce innumerable examples, but will content myself with only one, which occurred within the memory of our fathers. Messer Annibale Bentivogli, grandfather of the present Messer Annibale, being prince of Bologna, was murdered by the Canneschi, who had conspired against him, and there remained of his family one Messer Giovanni, who was still in his infancy. Immediately after the murder of Messer Annibale, the people rose and killed all the Canneschi. This was the consequence of the popularity which the Bentivogli enjoyed in those days in Bologna, and which went to that extent that after the death of Messer Annibale, when there remained not one of the family in Bologna capable of governing the state, the people received information that there was a Bentivogli in Florence who, until then, had been reputed the son of a blacksmith. They sent a deputation to him at Florence and conferred the government of the city upon him, which he exercised undisturbed until Messer Giovanni came to be of suitable age to assume it himself. I conclude, that a prince need apprehend but little from conspiracies, provided he possess the good will of his people, which is one of the most important points that a prince has to look to.

Amongst the well-organised and well-governed kingdoms of our time is that of France, which has a great many excellent institutions that secure the liberty and safety of the king. The most important of these is the parliament [parlement] and its authority; for the founder of that kingdom knew the ambition and insolence of the nobles, and judged it necessary to put a bit into their mouths with which to curb them. He knew at the same time the hatred of the mass of the people towards the nobles, based upon their fears. Wishing to secure both, and yet unwilling to make this the special care of the king, so as to relieve him of the responsibility to the nobles of seeming to favour the people, and to the people of favouring the nobles, he instituted the parliament to act as a judge, which might, without reference to the king, keep down the great, and favour the weak. Nor could there be a wiser system or one that affords more security to the king and his realm.

We may also draw another notable conclusion from this, namely, that princes should devolve all matters of responsibility upon others, and take upon themselves only those of grace. I conclude then anew, that a prince should treat his nobles with respect and consideration, and should avoid at the same time making himself odious to his people. It may perhaps seem to many that considering the life and death of many Roman emperors, their example contradicts my opinions, seeing that some who have led most exemplary lives, and displayed most noble qualities of the soul, yet lost the empire, or were even killed by their followers, who had conspired against them. I desire to meet this objection, and will therefore discuss the characters of some of those emperors, showing that the causes of their ruin were not different from those adduced by me above; and I will present some considerations that are important to the student of the history of those times. In this I shall confine myself to those emperors that succeeded one another from Marcus the philosopher to Maximinus; namely, Marcus, his son Commodus, Pertinax, Julian, Severus, Antoninus Caracalla his son, Macrinus, Heliogabalus, Alexander and Maximinus.

And I must remark at the outset, that where in other principalities the prince had to contend only with the ambition of the nobles and the insolence of the people, the Roman emperors had to meet a third difficulty, in having to bear with the cruelty and cupidity of the soldiers, which were so great that they caused the ruin of many, because of the difficulty of satisfying at the same time both the soldiers and the people; for the people love quiet, and for that reason they revere princes who are modest, whilst the soldiers love a prince of military spirit, and who is cruel, haughty and rapacious. And these qualities the prince must practise upon the people, so as to enable him to increase the pay of the soldiers, and to satisfy their avarice and cruelty. Whence it came that all those emperors were ruined who had not, by their natural or acquired qualities, the necessary influence that would enable them to restrain at the same time the soldiers and the people. Most of them, therefore, and especially those who had but recently attained the sovereignty, knowing the difficulty of satisfying two such different dispositions, sought rather to satisfy the soldiers, and cared but little about oppressing and offending the people. And this course was unavoidable for them; for inasmuch as princes generally cannot prevent being hated by some, they ought first of all to strive not to be hated by the mass of the people; but failing in this, they should by all means endeavour to avoid being hated by the more powerful. And therefore those emperors who, by reason of having but recently acquired the empire, had need of extraordinary favours, attached themselves more readily to the soldiery than to the people; which, however, was advantageous to them or not only according as such emperor knew how to maintain his ascendency over them. These were the reasons why Marcus, Pertinax and Alexander, being all three men of modest lives, lovers of justice, enemies to cruelty, humane and benevolent, came to a bad end, Marcus alone excepted, who lived and died much honoured; but he had succeeded to the empire by inheritance, and was not indebted for it either to the soldiers or to the favour of the people. He was, moreover, endowed with many virtues, which made him generally revered; and so long as he lived he always kept both the soldiery and the people within their proper bounds, and thus was neither hated nor contemned. But Pertinax was made emperor contrary to the will of the army, which, having been accustomed under Commodus to a life of unrestrained licence, could not bear the orderly life to which Pertinax wished to constrain them. Having thus incurred their hatred, to which disrespect became added on account of his age, he was ruined at the very outset of his reign. And here I would observe that hatred may be caused by good as well as by evil works, and therefore (as I have said above) a prince who wants to preserve his state is often obliged not to be good; for when the mass of the people or of the soldiery, or of the nobles, whose support is necessary for him, is corrupt, then it becomes the interest of the prince to indulge and satisfy their humour; and it is under such circumstances that good works will be injurious to him. Let us come now to Alexander, who was so good that, amongst other merits, it was said of him that during the fourteen years of his reign not one person was put to death by him without regular judicial proceedings. But being regarded as effeminate, and as allowing himself to be governed by his mother, he fell into disrespect, and the soldiery conspired against him and killed him.

Discussing now, by way of the opposite extreme, the qualities of Commodus, Severus, Antoninus Caracalla and Maximinus, we find them to have been most cruel and rapacious; and that, for the sake of keeping the soldiers satisfied, they did not hesitate to commit every kind of outrage upon the people; and that all of them, with exception of Septimius Severus, came to a bad end. The latter possessed such valour that although he imposed heavy burdens upon the people, yet, by keeping the soldiers his friends, he was enabled to reign undisturbed and happily; for his bravery caused him to be so much admired by the soldiers and the people that the latter were in a manner stupefied and astounded by it, whilst it made the former respectful and satisfied.

And as the actions of Severus were really great, considering that he was a prince of but recent date, I will show how well he knew to play the part of the fox and of the lion, whose natures a prince should be able to imitate, as I have shown above. Severus, knowing the indolence of the Emperor Julian, persuaded the troops which he commanded in Slavonia that it would be proper for them to go to Rome to avenge the death of Pertinax, who had been killed by the Imperial Guard. Under this pretext, without showing that he aspired to the Empire, he moved the army to Rome, and was in Italy before it was known even that he had started. On his arrival in Rome the senate, under the influence of fear, elected Severus emperor, Julian having previously been slain.

After this beginning, Severus had yet two difficulties to overcome before he could make himself master of the entire state: the one in Asia, where Niger, commander of the army of the East, had himself proclaimed emperor; and the other in the West, caused by Albinus, who also aspired to the empire. Deeming it dangerous to declare himself openly the enemy of both, Severus resolved to attack Niger and to deceive Albinus; and therefore he wrote to the latter that, having been elected emperor by the senate, he wished to share that dignity with him, and accordingly sent him the title of Caesar, and accepted him as his colleague, by resolution of the senate. Albinus received it all as truth; but after Severus had defeated and slain Niger, and quieted matters in the East, he returned to Rome and complained in the senate that Albinus, little grateful for the benefits which he had bestowed upon him, had plotted treason and murder against him, and that therefore it was incumbent upon him to go and punish this ingratitude and treason. Severus thereupon went into France to seek Albinus, and deprived him of his state and his life.

If now we examine minutely the conduct of Severus, we shall find that he combined the ferocity of the lion with the cunning of the fox, and that he was feared and revered by every one, and was not hated by the army. Nor ought we to be surprised to find that, although a new man, he yet should have been able to maintain himself at the head of so great an empire; for his eminent reputation saved him always from incurring the hatred of the people, which his rapacity might otherwise have provoked.

Antoninus Caracalla, the son of Severus, was also a man possessed of eminent qualities and rare gifts, which made him admired by the people and acceptable to the soldiery. For he was a military man, capable of enduring every fatigue, despising the delicacies of the table and every other effeminacy, which made him beloved by all the army. But his ferocity and cruelty were so great and unprecedented that, having on several occasions caused a large number of the people of Rome to be put to death, and at another time nearly the entire population of Alexandria, he became odious to the whole world, and began to be feared even by his immediate attendants, and finally was killed by a centurion in the midst of his army. Whence we may observe that princes cannot always escape assassination when prompted by a resolute and determined spirit; for any man who himself despises death can always inflict it upon others. But as men of this sort are rare, princes need not be very apprehensive about them; they should, however, be most careful not to offend grievously any of those who serve their persons, or who are around and near them in the service of the state. It was in this respect that Caracalla erred, for he had contumeliously slain a brother of a centurion, whom he had also threatened repeatedly, and yet kept him as one of his body-guard; which was a most reckless thing to do, and well calculated to prove ruinous to Antoninus Caracalla, as it finally did.

But we come now to Commodus, who might have kept the empire with great ease, having inherited it as the son of Marcus Aurelius. All he had to do was to follow in the footsteps of his father, which would have satisfied both the people and the army. But being of a cruel and bestial nature, he began by entertaining the army and making it licentious, so as to enable him the more freely to indulge his rapacity upon the people. And on the other hand he made himself contemptible in the eyes of his soldiers, by disregarding his own dignity, and descending into the arena to combat with gladiators, and doing other disgraceful things wholly unworthy of the imperial majesty. Being thus hated by the people and contemned by the army, a conspiracy was set on foot against him and he was killed.

It remains now for me to discuss the character of Maximinus. He was a most warlike man; and the army being tired of the effeminacy of Alexander Severus, of which I have spoken above, they elected Maximinus to the empire after the death of Alexander. But he did not retain it very long, for two circumstances made him both odious and despised. One was his extremely low origin, having been a shepherd in Thracia (which was generally known, and caused him to be held in great contempt by every one), and the other was his delay, when elected emperor, to go to Rome, there to take possession of the imperial throne. He had moreover earned the reputation of extreme cruelty, in consequence of the many acts of ferocity which he had committed through the agency of his prefects in Rome and elsewhere. Being thus despised by the whole world on account of his low origin, and on the other hand hated because of his cruelty, a conspiracy was formed against him, first in Africa, and then by the senate and people of Rome and all Italy. His army joined in the conspiracy, for being engaged in the siege of Aquileia and finding difficulty in taking it, they became tired of his harshness; and seeing that he had so many enemies, they lost their fear of him and put him to death.

I care not to discuss either Heliogabalus, or Macrinus, or Julian, who, being utterly contemptible, came quickly to an end; but will conclude this discourse by saying that the princes of our times are not subjected to the same difficulties in their governments by the extraordinary demands of their armies. For although they are obliged to show them some consideration, yet they are easily disposed of, as none of the sovereigns of the present day keep their armies constantly together, so as to become veterans in the service of the government and the administration of the provinces, as was the case in the time of the Roman Empire. And if in those days it was necessary to have more regard to the armies than to the people, because of their greater power, it nowadays behooves princes rather to keep the people contented, for they have more influence and power than the soldiers. The Grand Turk and the Sultan of Egypt form an exception to this rule, for the Turk always keeps himself surrounded by twelve thousand infantry and fifteen thousand cavalry, on which the strength and security of his empire depends; he must therefore keep these troops devoted to himself, regardless of all consideration for the people.

It is much the same with the government of the Sultan of Egypt, which being entirely under the control of the army, it behooves him also, regardless of the people, to keep the soldiery his friends. And here I would remark that the government of the Sultan of Egypt differs from all other principalities, although in some respects similar to the Christian Pontificate, which cannot be called either an hereditary or a new principality. For when the Sultan dies, his sons do not inherit the government, but it devolves upon whoever is elected to that dignity by those who have authority in the matter. And as this system is consecrated by time, it cannot be called a new principality; for it is free from all the difficulties that appertain to new principalities. For even if the prince be new, the institutions of the state are old, and are so organised as to receive the elected the same as though he were their hereditary lord.

But to return to our subject, I say that whoever reflects carefully upon the above discourse will find that the ruin of the above-mentioned emperors was caused by either hatred or contempt; and he will also see how it happened that, whilst some of them having proceeded one way and some in the opposite, in some instances the one had a happy, and the other an unhappy end. For in the case of Pertinax and Alexander, both being new princes, it was useless and dangerous for them to attempt to imitate Marcus, who had inherited the empire. And in the same way it was ruinous for Caracalla, Commodus and Maximinus to imitate Severus, for neither of them possessed the noble qualities necessary to enable them to follow in his footsteps.

A prince, therefore, who has but recently acquired his principality, cannot imitate the conduct of Marcus Aurelius; nor is it necessary for him to imitate that of Septimius Severus. But he should learn from Severus what is necessary to found a state, and from Marcus what is proper and glorious for the preservation of a state that is already firmly established.

CHAPTER 20

Whether the erection of fortresses, and many other things which princes often do, are useful or injurious

Some princes, with a view to a more secure tenure of their states, have disarmed their subjects; some have kept the countries subject to them divided into different parties; others have purposely encouraged enmities against themselves; whilst others again have endeavoured to win the good will of those whom in the beginning of their reign they suspected of hostile feelings. Some have built fortresses, whilst others have demolished and razed those that existed. Now although I cannot pronounce any definite judgment as to these different ways of proceeding, without examining the particular condition of those states where similar proceedings are to be applied, yet I will treat the subject in that general way of which it is susceptible.

It has never happened that a new prince has disarmed his subjects; on the contrary rather, if he has found them unarmed, he has armed them, and in that way has made them as it were his own, and made those faithful who before were suspect; whilst those who were loyal to him before will remain so, and thus he will convert his subjects into his partisans and supporters. And although a prince cannot arm all his subjects, yet by giving certain advantages to those whom he does arm, he secures himself the better against the others who are not armed, and who will excuse the preference shown to those whom the prince has armed and thereby laid under obligations to himself. For the others will excuse him, and will recognise the necessity of rewarding those who are exposed to greater danger, and who have more onerous duties to perform.

But a prince who disarms his subjects will at once offend them, by thus showing that he has no confidence in them, but that he suspects them either of cowardice or want of loyalty, and this will cause them to hate him. And as the prince cannot remain without an armed force, he will have to resort to mercenaries, the objections to which I have fully set forth in a preceding chapter. And even if these mercenaries were not absolutely bad, they would still be insufficient to protect the prince against powerful enemies and suspected subjects. Therefore, as I have said, new princes should always establish armed forces in their newly acquired principalities; for which history furnishes us abundance of precedents.

But when a prince acquires a new state, which he annexes as an appendage to his old possessions, then it is advisable for him to disarm the inhabitants of the new state, excepting those who, upon the acquisition of the same, declared in the prince's favour. But even these it will be well for him to weaken and enervate when occasion offers; so that his armed forces shall be organised in such a way as to consist entirely of his own subjects, natives of his original state.

Our ancestors, and those who were regarded as wise, used to say that the way to hold Pistoia was through party divisions, and Pisa by means of fortresses. Accordingly they encouraged such party divisions in some of the towns that were subject to them, for the purpose of holding them the more easily. This may have been very well in those times when the different powers of Italy were to some extent evenly balanced; but it does not seem to me that such a precept is applicable at the present day, for I do not believe that party divisions purposely made are ever productive of good. To the contrary rather, cities divided against themselves are easily lost, on the approach of an enemy; for the weaker party will always unite with the external foe, and then the other will not be able to maintain itself.

The Venetians, influenced I believe by the above reasons, encouraged the feuds between the Guelphs and the Ghibellines in the cities that were subject to them; and although they never allowed them to come to bloody conflicts, yet they fomented their quarrels sufficiently to keep the citizens occupied with their own dissensions, so that they could not turn against the Venetians. This, however, did not result as they had designed, for after the defeat at Vaila one of the parties promptly took courage, and deprived the Venetians of the entire state. Measures of this kind, therefore, argue weakness in a prince, for a strong government will never allow such divisions: they can be of advantage only in time of peace, as by their means subjects may be more easily managed, but in case of war the fallacy of this system becomes manifest. Princes undoubtedly become great by overcoming all difficulties and oppositions that may spring up against them; and therefore does Fortune, when she intends to make a new prince great (for whom it is more important to acquire a reputation than for an hereditary prince), cause enemies to arise and make attempts against the prince, so as to afford him the opportunity of overcoming them, and that he may thus rise higher by means of the very ladder which his enemies have brought against him. And therefore the opinion has been held by many, that a wise prince should, when opportunity offers, adroitly nurse some enmities against himself, so that by overcoming them his greatness may be increased.

Princes, and more especially new ones, have often met with more fidelity and devotion in the very men whom at the beginning of their reign they mistrusted, than in those upon whom they at first confidently relied. Thus Pandolfo Petrucci, prince of Siena, governed his state more by the aid of those whom he at first regarded with suspicion, than by that of any of his other subjects. But no general rules can be laid down for this, as the prince must in this respect be governed by circumstances. I will only observe that those men who at the beginning of a prince's reign are hostile to him, and who are yet so situated that they need his support for their maintenance, will always be most easily won over by him; and they will be obliged to continue to serve him with the greater fidelity, because of the importance of their effacing by their good conduct the bad opinion which the prince had formed of them at the beginning. And thus the prince will derive more useful service from these than from such as from over confidence in their security will serve his interests negligently.

And since the subject requires it, I will not omit to remind the prince who has but recently acquired a state by the favour of its citizens to consider well the reasons that influenced those who favoured his success. For if it was not a natural affection for him, but merely their dissatisfaction with the previous government, then he will have much trouble and difficulty in preserving their attachment, for it will be almost impossible for the prince to satisfy their expectations. Now if we carefully study the reasons of this from the examples which both ancient and modern history furnish us, we shall find that it is much easier for a prince to win the friendship of those who previous to his acquisition of the state were content with its government, and who must therefore have been hostile to him, than of those who, from being malcontents under the previous government, became his friends, and favoured his seizing the state.

It has been the general practice of princes, for the purpose of holding their states securely, to build fortresses to serve as a curb and check upon those who might make an attempt against the government, and at the same time to afford the prince a secure place of refuge against the first attack. I approve of this system, because it was practised by the ancients; and yet we have seen in our own times that Messer Niccolò Vitelli dismantled two fortresses in Città di Castello, so as to enable him to hold that place. Guidobaldo, Duke of Urbino, on returning to his state, whence he had been driven by Cesare Borgia, razed all the fortresses of that province to their very foundations; for he thought that it would be more difficult for him to lose that state a second time without those fortresses. The Bentivogli did the same thing on their return to Bologna. Fortresses then are useful or not, according to circumstances; and whilst in one way they are advantageous, they may in another prove injurious to a prince. The question may therefore be stated thus. A prince who fears his own people more than he does foreigners should build fortresses; but he who has more cause to fear strangers than his own people should do without them. The citadel of Milan, built by Francesco Sforza, has caused, and will yet cause, more trouble to the house of Sforza than any other disturbance in that state. The best fortress which a prince can possess is the affection of his people; for even if he have fortresses, and is hated by his people, the fortresses will not save him; for when a people have once risen in arms against their prince, there will be no lack of strangers who will aid them.

In our own times we have seen but one instance where fortresses have been of advantage to a ruler, and that was the case of the Countess of Fourli, when her husband, the Count Girolamo, was killed; for the castle of Fourli enabled her to escape from the fury of the people, and there to await assistance from Milan, so as to recover her state, the circumstances at the time being such that the people could not obtain assistance from strangers. Later, however, when she was assailed by Cesare Borgia, the people of Fourli, being hostile to her, united with the stranger, and then the castle was no longer of any great value to her. Thus she would have been more secure if she had not been hated by her people, than she was in possessing the castle.

After a full examination of the question, then, I approve of those who build fortresses, as well as those who do not. But I blame all those who, in their confident reliance upon such strongholds, do not mind incurring the hatred of their own people.

CHAPTER 21

How princes should conduct themselves to acquire a reputation

Nothing makes a prince so much esteemed as the undertaking of great enterprises and the setting a noble example in his own person. We have a striking instance of this in Ferdinand of Aragon, the present King of Spain. He may be called, as it were, a new prince; for, from being king of a feeble state, he has, by his fame and glory, become the first sovereign of Christendom; and if we examine his actions we shall find them all most grand, and some of them extraordinary. In the beginning of his reign he attacked Granada, and it was this undertaking that was the very foundation of his greatness. At first he carried on this war leisurely and without fear of opposition; for he kept the nobles of Castile occupied with this enterprise, and their minds being thus engaged by war, they gave no attention to the innovations introduced by the king, who thereby acquired a reputation and an influence over the nobles without their being aware of it. The money of the Church and of the people enabled him to support his armies, and by that long war he succeeded in giving a stable foundation to his military establishment, which afterwards brought him so much honour. Besides this, to be able to engage in still greater enterprises, he always availed himself of religion as a pretext, and committed a pious cruelty in spoliating and driving the Moors out of his kingdom, which certainly was a most admirable and extraordinary example. Under the same cloak of religion he attacked Africa, and made a descent upon Italy, and finally assailed France. And thus he was always planning great enterprises, which kept the minds of his subjects in a state of suspense and admiration, and occupied with their results. And these different enterprises followed so quickly one upon the other, that he never gave men a chance deliberately to make any attempt against himself.

It is also important for a prince to give striking examples of his interior administration (similar to those that are related of Messer Bernabo di Milano), when an occasion presents itself to reward or punish any one who has in civil affairs either rendered great service to the state, or committed some crime, so that it may be much talked about. But, above all, a prince should endeavour to invest all his actions with a character of grandeur and excellence. A prince, furthermore, becomes esteemed when he shows himself either a true friend or a real enemy; that is, when, regardless of consequences, he declares himself openly for or against another, which will always be more creditable to him than to remain neutral. For if two of your neighbouring potentates should come to war amongst themselves, they are either of such character that when one of them has been defeated, you will have cause to fear the conqueror, or not. In either case, it will always be better for you to declare yourself openly and make fair war; for if you fail to do so, you will be very apt to fall a prey to the victor, to the delight and satisfaction of the defeated party, and you will have no claim for protection or assistance from either the one or the other. For the conqueror will want no doubtful friends, who did not stand by him in time of trial; and the defeated party will not forgive you for having refused, with arms in hand, to take the chance of his fortunes.

When Antiochus came into Greece, having been sent by the Aetolians to drive out the Romans, he sent ambassadors to the Achaeans, who were friends of the Romans, to induce them to remain neutral; whilst the Romans, on the other hand, urged them to take up arms in their behalf. When the matter came up for deliberation in the council of the Achaeans, and the ambassadors of Antiochus endeavoured to persuade them to remain neutral, the Roman legate replied: 'As to the course which is said to be the best and most advantageous for your state, not to intervene in our war, I can assure you that the very reverse will be the case; for by not intervening you will, without thanks and without credit, remain a prize to the victor.'

And it will always be the case that he who is not your friend will claim neutrality at your hands, whilst your friend will ask your armed intervention in his favour. Irresolute princes, for the sake of avoiding immediate danger, adopt most frequently the course of neutrality, and are generally ruined in consequence. But when a prince declares himself boldly in favour of one party, and that party proves victorious, even though the victor be powerful, and you are at his discretion, yet is he bound to you in love and obligation; and men are never so base as to repay these by such flagrant ingratitude as the oppressing you under these circumstances would be.

Moreover, victories are never so complete as to dispense the victor from all regard for justice. But when the party whom you have supported loses, then he will ever after receive you as a friend, and, when able, will assist you in turn; and thus you will have become the sharer of a fortune which in time may be retrieved.

In the second case, when the contending parties are such that you need not fear the victor, then it is the more prudent to give him your support; for you thereby aid one to ruin the other, whom he should save if he were wise; for although he has defeated his adversary, yet he remains at your discretion, inasmuch as without your assistance victory would have been impossible for him. And here it should be noted, that a prince ought carefully to avoid making common cause with any one more powerful than himself, for the purpose of attacking another power, unless he should be compelled to do so by necessity. For if the former is victorious, then you are at his mercy; and princes should, if possible, avoid placing themselves in such a position.

The Venetians allied themselves with France against the Duke of Milan, an alliance which they could easily have avoided, and which proved their ruin. But when it is unavoidable, as was the case with the Florentines when Spain and the Pope united their forces to attack Lombardy, then a prince ought to join the stronger party, for the reasons above given. Nor is it to be supposed that a state can ever adopt a course that is entirely safe; on the contrary, a prince must make up his mind to take the chance of all the doubts and uncertainties; for such is the order of things that one inconvenience cannot be avoided except at the risk of being exposed to another. And it is the province of prudence to discriminate amongst these inconveniences, and to accept the least evil for good.

A prince should also show himself a lover of virtue, and should honour all who excel in any one of the arts, and should encourage his citizens quietly to pursue their vocations, whether of commerce, agriculture or any other human industry; so that the one may not abstain from embellishing his possessions for fear of their being taken from him, nor the other from opening new sources of commerce for fear of taxes. But the prince should provide rewards for those who are willing to do these things, and for all who strive to enlarge his city or state. And besides this, he should at suitable periods amuse his people with festivities and spectacles. And as cities are generally divided into guilds and classes, he should keep account of these bodies, and occasionally be present at their assemblies, and should set an example of his affability and magnificence; preserving, however, always the majesty of his dignity, which should never be wanting on any occasion or under any circumstances.

CHAPTER 22

Of the ministers of princes

The choice of his ministers is of no slight importance to a prince; they are either good or not, according as the prince himself is sagacious or otherwise; and upon the character of the persons with whom a prince surrounds himself depends the first impression that is formed of his own ability. If his ministers and counsellors are competent and faithful, he will be reputed wise, because he had known how to discern their capacity and how to secure their fidelity; but if they prove otherwise, then the opinion formed of the prince will not be favourable, because of his want of judgment in their first selection. Every one who knew Messer Antonio di Venafro as the minister of Pandolfo Petrucci, prince of Siena, judged Pandolfo to be a man of great sagacity in having chosen Messer Antonio for his minister.

There are three sorts of intellect: the one understands things by its own quickness of perception; another understands them when explained by some one else; and the third understands them neither by itself nor by the explanation of others. The first is the best, the second very good, and the third useless. Now we must admit that Pandolfo did not belong to the first order, but rather to the second. For whenever a prince has the sagacity to recognise the good or the evil that is said or done, he will, even without being a genius, be able to judge whether the minister's actions are good or bad; and he will praise the one and censure the other. And thus the minister, seeing that he cannot hope to deceive the prince, will continue to serve him faithfully. But the true way for a prince to know his minister is as follows, and never fails. Whenever he sees that the minister thinks more of himself than of the prince, and that in all his doings he seeks his own advantage more than that of the state, then the prince may be sure that that man will never be a good minister, and is not to be trusted. For a man who has the administration of a state in his hands, should never think of himself, but only of the prince, and should never bring anything to his notice that does not relate to the interest of the government.

On the other hand, the prince, by way of securing the devotion of his minister, should think of him and bind him to himself by obligations; he should bestow riches upon him, and should share the honours as well as the cares with him; so that the abundance of honours and riches conferred by the prince upon his minister may cause the latter not to desire either the one or the other from any other source, and that the weight of cares may make him dread a change, knowing that without the prince he could not sustain it. And when the relations between the prince and his minister are thus constituted, they will be able to confide in each other; but if they be otherwise, then one or the other of them will surely come to a bad end.

CHAPTER 23

How to avoid flatterers

I will not leave unnoticed an important subject, and an evil against which princes have much difficulty in defending themselves, if they are not extremely prudent, or have not made good choice of ministers; and this relates to flatterers, who abound in all courts. Men are generally so well pleased with themselves and their own acts, and delude themselves to such a degree, that it is with difficulty they escape from the pest of flatterers; and in their efforts to avoid them they expose themselves to the risk of being contemned. There is no other way of guarding against adulation, than to make people understand that they will not offend you by speaking the truth. On the other hand, when every one feels at liberty to tell you the truth, they will be apt to be lacking in respect to you. A prudent prince therefore should follow a middle course, choosing for ministers of his government only wise men, and to these only should he give full power to tell him the truth, and they should only be allowed to speak to him of those things which he asks of them, and of none other. But then the prince should ask them about everything, and should listen to their opinions and reflect upon them, and afterwards form his own resolutions. And he should bear himself towards all his advisers in such manner that each may know that the more freely he speaks, the more acceptable will he be. But outside of these he should not listen to any one, but follow the course agreed upon, and be firm in his resolves. Whoever acts otherwise will either be misled by his flatterers, or will vacillate in his decisions, because of the variety of opinions; and this will naturally result in his losing in public estimation.

I will cite one modern example to this effect. Padre Luca, in the service of the present Emperor Maximilian, in speaking of his

Majesty, says that he 'counsels with no one, and yet never does anything in his own way'; which results from his following the very opposite course to that above indicated; for the emperor is a reserved man, who never communicates his secrets to any one, nor takes advice from anybody. But when he attempts to carry his plans into execution and they begin to be known, then also do they begin to be opposed by those whom he has around him; and being easily influenced, he is diverted from his own resolves. And thence it comes that he undoes one day what he has done the day before, and that one never knows what he wants or designs to do; and therefore his conclusions cannot be depended upon.

A prince nevertheless should always take counsel, but only when he wants it, and not when others wish to thrust it upon him; in fact, he should rather discourage persons from tendering him advice unsolicited by him. But he should be an extensive questioner, and a patient listener to the truth respecting the things inquired about, and should even show his anger in case any one should, for some reason, not tell him the truth.

Those who imagine that a prince who has the reputation of sagacity is not indebted for it to his own natural gifts, but to the good counsels of those who surround him, certainly deceive themselves. For it may be taken as a general and infallible rule, that a prince who is not naturally wise cannot be well advised, unless he should perchance place himself entirely in the hands of one man, who should guide him in all things, and who would have to be a man of uncommon ability. In such a case a prince might be well directed, but it would probably not last long, because his counsellor would in a short time deprive him of his state. But a prince who is not wise himself, and counsels with more than one person, will never have united counsels; for he will himself lack the ability to harmonise and combine the various counsels and suggestions. His advisers will only think of their own advantage, which the prince will neither know how to discern nor how to correct.

And things cannot well be otherwise, for men will always naturally prove bad, unless some necessity constrains them to be good. Whence we conclude that good counsels, no matter whence they may come, result wholly from the prince's own sagacity; but the wisdom of the prince never results from good counsels.

CHAPTER 24

The reason why the princes of Italy have
lost their states

A judicious observation of the above-given rules will cause a new prince to be regarded as though he were an hereditary one, and will very soon make him more firm and secure in his state than if he had grown old in its possession. For the actions of a new prince are much more closely observed and scrutinised than those of an hereditary one; and when they are known to be virtuous, they will win the confidence and affections of men much more for the new prince, and make his subjects feel under greater obligations to him, than if he were of the ancient line. For men are ever more taken with the things of the present than with those of the past; and when they find their own good in the present, then they enjoy it and seek none other, and will be ready in every way to defend the new prince, provided he be not wanting to himself in other respects. And thus he will have the double glory of having established a new principality, and of having strengthened and adorned it with good laws, good armies, good allies and good examples. And in the same way will it be a double shame to an hereditary prince, if through want of prudence and ability he loses his state.

If now we examine the conduct of those princes of Italy who in our day have lost their states, such as the King of Naples, the Duke of Milan and others, we shall note in them at once a common defect as regards their military forces, for the reasons which we have discussed at length above. And we shall also find that in some instances the people were hostile to the prince; or if he had the good will of the people, he knew not how to conciliate that of the nobles. For unless there be some such defects as these, states are not lost when the prince has energy enough to keep an army in the field.

Philip of Macedon, not the father of Alexander the Great, but he who was vanquished by Titus Quinctius, had not much of a state as compared with Rome and Greece, who attacked him; yet being a military man, and at the same time knowing how to preserve the good will of the people and to assure himself of the support of the nobles, he sustained the war against the Romans and Greeks for many years; and although he finally lost some cities, yet he preserved his kingdom.

Those of our princes, therefore, who have lost their dominions after having been established in them for many years, should not blame fortune, but only their own indolence and lack of energy; for in times of quiet they never thought of the possibility of a change (it being a common defect of men in fair weather to take no thought of storms), and afterwards, when adversity overtook them, their first impulse was to fly, and not to defend themselves, hoping that the people, when disgusted with the insolence of the victors, would recall them. Such a course may be very well when others fail, but it is very discreditable to neglect other means for it that might have saved you from ruin; for no one ever falls deliberately, in the expectation that some one will help him up, which either does not happen, or, if it does, will not contribute to your security; for it is a base thing to look to others for your defence instead of depending upon yourself. That defence alone is effectual, sure and durable which depends upon yourself and your own valour.

CHAPTER 25

Of the influence of fortune in human affairs, and how it may be counteracted

I am well aware that many have held and still hold the opinion, that the affairs of this world are so controlled by fortune and by the divine power that human wisdom and foresight cannot modify them; that, in fact, there is no remedy against the decrees of fate, and that therefore it is not worth while to make any effort, but to yield unconditionally to the power of fortune. This opinion has been generally accepted in our times, because of the great changes that have taken place, and are still being witnessed every day, and are beyond all human conjecture.

In reflecting upon this at times, I am myself in some measure inclined to that belief; nevertheless, as our free will is not entirely destroyed, I judge that it may be assumed as true that fortune to the extent of one half is the arbiter of our actions, but that she permits us to direct the other half, or perhaps a little less, ourselves. I compare this to a swollen river, which in its fury overflows the plains, tears up the trees and buildings, and sweeps the earth from one place and deposits it in another. Every one flies before the flood, and yields to its fury, unable to resist it; and notwithstanding this state of things, men do not when the river is in its ordinary condition provide against its overflow by dikes and walls, so that when it rises it may flow either in the channel thus provided for it, or that at any rate its violence may not be entirely unchecked, nor its effects prove so injurious. It is the same with fortune, who displays her power where there is no organised valour to resist her, and where she knows that there are no dikes or walls to control her.

If now you examine Italy, which is the seat of the changes under consideration, and has occasioned their occurrence, you will see that she is like an open country, without dikes or any other protection against inundations; and that if she had been protected with proper valour and wisdom, as is the case with Germany, Spain and France, these inundations would either not have caused the great changes which they did, or they would not have occurred at all.

These remarks I deem sufficient as regards resisting fortune in general; but confining myself now more to particular cases, I say that we see a prince fortunate one day, and ruined the next, without his nature or any of his qualities being changed. I believe this results mainly from the causes which have been discussed at length above; namely, that the prince who relies entirely upon fortune will be ruined according as fortune varies. I believe, further, that the prince who conforms his conduct to the spirit of the times will be fortunate; and in the same way will he be unfortunate if in his actions he disregards the spirit of the times. For we see men proceed in various ways to attain the end they aim at, such as glory and riches: the one with circumspection, the other with rashness; one with violence, another with cunning; one with patience, and another with impetuosity; and all may succeed in their different ways. We also see that, of two men equally prudent, the one will accomplish his designs, whilst the other fails; and in the same way we see two men succeed equally well by two entirely different methods, the one being prudent and the other rash; which is due to nothing else than the character of the times, to which they either conform in their proceedings or not. Whence it comes, as I have said, that two men by entirely different modes of action will achieve the same results; whilst of two others, proceeding precisely in the same way, the one will accomplish his end, and the other not. This also causes the difference of success; for if one man, acting with caution and patience, is also favoured by time and circumstances, he will be successful; but if these change, then will he be ruined, unless, indeed, he changes his conduct accordingly. Nor is there any man so sagacious that he will always know how to conform to such change of times and circumstances; for men do not readily deviate from the course to which their nature inclines them; and moreover, if they have generally been prosperous by following one course, they cannot persuade themselves that it would be well to depart from it. Thus the cautious man, when the moment comes for him to strike a bold blow, will not know how to do it, and thence will he fail; whilst, if he could have changed his nature with the times and circumstances, his usual good fortune would not have abandoned him.

Pope Julius II was in all his actions most impetuous; and the times and circumstances happened so conformably to that mode of proceeding that he always achieved happy results. Witness the first attempt he made upon Bologna, when Messer Giovanni Bentivogli was still living. This attempt gave umbrage to the Venetians, and also to the kings of Spain and France who held a conference on the subject. But Pope Julius, with his habitual boldness and impetuosity, assumed the direction of that expedition in person; which caused the Spaniards and the Venetians to remain quiet in suspense, the latter from fear, and the others from a desire to recover the entire kingdom of Naples. On the other hand, the Pope drew the King of France after him; for that king, seeing that Julius had already started on the expedition, and wishing to gain his friendship for the purpose of humbling the Venetians, judged that he could not refuse him the assistance of his army without manifest injury to himself.

Pope Julius II, then, achieved by this impetuous movement what no other pontiff could have accomplished with all possible human prudence. For had he waited to start from Rome until all his plans were definitely arranged, and everything carefully organised, as every other pontiff would have done, he would certainly never have succeeded; for the king would have found a thousand excuses, and the others would have caused him a thousand apprehensions. I will not dwell upon the other actions of Julius II, which were all of a similar character, and have all succeeded equally well. The shortness of his life saved him from experiencing any reverses; for if times had supervened that would have made it necessary for him to proceed with caution and prudence, he would assuredly have been ruined; for he could never have deviated from the course to which his nature inclined him.

I conclude, then, inasmuch as fortune is changeable, that men who persist obstinately in their own ways will be successful only so long as those ways coincide with those of fortune; and whenever these differ, they fail. But, on the whole, I judge impetuosity to be better than caution; for fortune is a woman, and if you wish to master her, you must strike and beat her, and you will see that she allows herself to be more easily vanquished by the rash and the violent than by those who proceed more slowly and coldly. And therefore, as a woman, she ever favours youth more than age, for youth is less cautious and more energetic, and commands fortune with greater audacity.

CHAPTER 26

Exhortation to deliver Italy from foreign barbarians

Reviewing now all I have said in the foregoing discourses, and thinking to myself that, if the present time should be favourable for Italy to receive and honour a new prince, and the opportunity were given to a prudent and virtuous man to establish a new form of government that would bring honour to himself and happiness to the mass of the Italian people, so many things would combine for the advantage of such a new prince, that, so far as I know, no previous time was ever more favourable for such a change. And if, as I have said, it was necessary for the purpose of displaying the virtue of Moses that the people of Israel should be held in bondage in Egypt; and that the Persians should be opposed to the Medes, so as to bring to light the greatness and courage of Cyrus; and that the Athenians should be dispersed for the purpose of illustrating the excellence of Theseus; so at present, for the purpose of making manifest the virtues of one Italian spirit, it was necessary that Italy should have been brought to her present condition of being in a worse bondage than that of the Jews, more enslaved than the Persians, more scattered than the Athenians, without a head, without order, vanquished and despoiled, lacerated, overrun by her enemies, and subjected to every kind of devastation.

And although, up to the present time, there may have been some one who may have given a gleam of hope that he was ordained by Heaven to redeem Italy, yet have we seen how, in the very zenith of his career, he was so checked by fortune that poor Italy remained as it were lifeless, and waiting to see who might be chosen to heal her wounds – to put an end to her devastation, to the sacking of Lombardy, to the spoliation and ruinous taxation of

the kingdom of Naples and of Tuscany – and who should heal her
sores that have festered so long. You see how she prays God that
he may send some one who shall redeem her from this cruelty and
barbarous insolence. You see her eagerly disposed to follow any
banner, provided there be some one to bear it aloft. But there is
no one at present in whom she could place more hope than in
your illustrious house, O magnificent Lorenzo! Which, with its
virtue and fortune, favoured by God and the Church of which it is
now the head, could make an effectual beginning of her
deliverance. And this will not be difficult for you, if you will first
study carefully the lives and actions of the men whom I have
named above. And although these men were rare and wonderful,
they were nevertheless but men, and the opportunities which they
had were far less favourable than the present; nor were their
undertakings more just or more easy than this; neither were they
more favoured by the Almighty than you are. Here, then, is great
justice; for war is just when it is necessary, and a resort to arms
is beneficent when there is no hope in anything else. The
opportunity is most favourable, and when that is the case there can
be no great difficulties, provided you follow the course of those
whom I have held up to you as examples. Although in their case
extraordinary things, without parallel, were brought about by the
hand of God – the sea divided for their passage, a pillar of cloud
pointed their way through the wilderness, the rock poured forth
water to assuage their thirst, and it rained manna to appease their
hunger – yet your greatness combines all, and on your own efforts
will depend the result. God will not do everything; for that would
deprive us of our free will, and of that share of glory which
belongs to us.

Nor should we wonder that not one of the Italians whom I have
mentioned has been able to accomplish that which it is to be
hoped will be done by your illustrious house; for if in so many
revolutions in Italy, and in the conduct of so many wars, it would
seem that military capacity and valour have become extinct, it is
owing to the fact that the old military system was defective, and
no one has come forward capable of establishing a new one. And
nothing brings a man who has newly risen so much honour as the
establishing of new laws and institutions of his own creation; if
they have greatness in them and become well established, they

will make the prince admired and revered; and there is no lack of opportunity in Italy for the introduction of every kind of reform. The people have great courage, provided it be not wanting in their leaders. Look but at their single combats, and their encounters when there are but a few on either side, and see how superior the Italians have shown themselves in strength, dexterity and ability. But when it comes to their armies, then these qualities do not appear, because of the incapacity of the chiefs, who cannot enforce obedience from those who are versed in the art of war, and every one believes himself to be so; for up to the present time there have been none so decidedly superior in valour and good fortune that the others yielded him obedience. Thence it comes that in so great a length of time, and in the many wars that have occurred within the past twenty years, the armies, whenever wholly composed of Italians, have given but poor account of themselves. Witness first Taro, then Alessandria, Capua, Genoa, Vaila, Bologna and Mestre.

If, then, your illustrious house is willing to follow the examples of those distinguished men who have redeemed their countries, you will before anything else, and as the very foundation of every enterprise, have to provide yourself with a national army. And you cannot have more faithful, truer and better soldiers than the Italians. And whilst each individual is good, they will become still better when they are all united, and know that they are commanded by their own prince, who will honour and support them. It is necessary, therefore, to provide troops of this kind, so as to be able successfully to oppose Italian valour to the attacks of foreigners.

And although the infantry of the Swiss and of the Spaniards is looked upon as terrible, yet both of them have a defect, which will permit a third organisation not only to resist them, but confidently hope to vanquish them. For the Spaniards cannot withstand the shock of the cavalry, and the Swiss dread infantry when they encounter it in battle as obstinate as themselves. Whence we have seen, what further experience will prove more fully, that the Spaniards cannot resist the French cavalry, and that the Swiss succumb to the Spanish infantry. And although we have not yet had a full trial of the latter, yet have we had a fair specimen of it in the battle of Ravenna, where the Spaniards with great agility, and protected by their bucklers, rushed under the pikes of the Germans, and were thus able to attack them securely without the Germans being able to prevent it; and had it not been for the cavalry which fell upon the Spaniards, they might have destroyed the entire German infantry.

Knowing, then, the defects of the one and the other of these systems of infantry, you can organise a new one that shall avoid these defects, and shall be able to resist cavalry as well as infantry. And this is to be done, not by a change of arms, but by an entirely different organisation and discipline. This is one of the things which, if successfully introduced, will give fame and greatness to a new prince.

You must not, then, allow this opportunity to pass, so that Italy, after waiting so long, may at last see her deliverer appear. Nor can I possibly express with what affection he would be received in all those provinces that have suffered so long from this inundation of foreign foes – with what thirst for vengeance, with what persistent faith, with what devotion and with what tears! What door would be closed to him? Who would refuse him obedience? What envy would dare oppose him? What Italian would refuse him homage? This barbarous dominion of the foreigner offends the very nostrils of everybody!

Let your illustrious house, then, assume this task with that courage and hopefulness which every just enterprise inspires; so that under your banner our country may recover its ancient fame, and under your auspices may be verified the words of Petrarch –

> Virtù contro al furore
> Prenderà l'arme, e fia il combatter corto;
> Chè l'antico valore
> Negli Italici cuor non è ancor morto.
>
> Canz. XVI. v. 93-96

> Virtue against fury shall advance the fight,
> And it in the combat soon shall put to flight;
> For the old Roman valour is not dead,
> Nor in the Italians breasts extinguishèd.
>
> (Trans. Edward Dacres, 1640)

The History of Florence*

The year 1498 was full of many grave and varied events which opened with the downfall of Fra Girolamo. He had stopped preaching on the orders of the Signoria [ruling body], and just when the violent persecution he suffered from both clerics and laymen seemed to have died down, a small incident gave rise to a complete reversal of his fortunes. About two years before, when preaching in Santa Liperata, Fra Domenico da Pescia, his companion in the Order of San Marco, who was a simple man with a reputation for living a saintly life and who followed Fra Girolamo's style in predicting future events in his sermons, had said that if it were necessary to prove the truth of what they foretold, they would revive a corpse and walk through fire unharmed through God's grace; and Fra Girolamo had later repeated this. Nothing had been said about this since, until one Fra Francesco of the Franciscan Order, who preached in Santa Croce and loathed Fra Girolamo and all his works, began to say in his sermons that to prove how false these were he was willing to walk through fire in the Piazza de' Signori if Fra Girolamo would do so too. He added that he was sure he would burn, but so would Fra Girolamo, and this would prove that there was no truth in him, as he had so often boasted that he would issue unhurt from the fire. Fra Domenico was told of this while he was preaching instead of Fra Girolamo; and so he accepted the challenge in the pulpit, offering not Fra Girolamo but himself for this experiment.

---

* F. Guicciardini, *The History of Florence*, ed. J. R. Hale, trans. C. Grayson, New English Library, London 1966. Extract from chapter 16.

This pleased many citizens of both parties who wished these divisions to end and all the uncertainties to be settled once and for all. They began to negotiate with the two preachers about putting the trial into effect. Finally after much argument all the friars agreed that a fire should be lit, and for Fra Girolamo a friar of his Order should enter it, the choice of the representative being left to him. Likewise for the other side a Franciscan friar should be nominated by his superiors. Having decided also on the date, Fra Girolamo had permission from the Signoria to preach; and preaching in San Marco he showed the great importance of miracles and said that they should not be used except in dire necessity when reasoning and experience proved insufficient; as the Christian faith had been proved in infinitely varied ways, and the truth of the things he had predicted had been shown with such effect and reason that anyone who was not hardened in wickedness could understand them, he had not had recourse to miracles so as not to tempt God. Nevertheless, since they had now been challenged, they willingly accepted, and all could be sure that on entering the fire the result would be that their friar would come out alive and unharmed while the other would be burned. If the opposite happened, they might freely say that he had preached lies. He added that not only his friars but anyone who entered the fire in defence of this truth would have the same experience. And then he asked them whether, if need be, they would go through fire to support the cause of so great a work ordered by God. With a great cry nearly everyone present answered that they would. An amazing thing to think of, because without any doubt, if Fra Girolamo had told them to, very many would indeed have gone through fire. Finally on the appointed day, the 27 of April, which was the Saturday before Palm Sunday, a platform was set up in the middle of the Piazza de' Signori with a great bonfire of faggots. The Franciscans came at the appointed time and went into the loggia of the Signoria; and then the Dominican friars arrived, many of them robed, singing the psalm *Exsurgat Dominus et dissipentur inimici eius* [the Lord shall arise and his enemies be scattered], and with them Fra Girolamo bearing the Host, in honour of which some friars and many lay-followers carried lighted torches. Their procession was so devout and showed so clearly that they came to the trial with the highest courage, that it not only reassured their own followers but even made their enemies flinch.

When they had entered the loggia, separated however from the Franciscans by a wooden partition, some difficulty arose about the clothes Fra Domenico da Pescia was to wear to walk through he fire. The Franciscans were afraid they might be enchanted. As they could not agree the Signoria repeatedly sent two citizens from each party to discuss their differences: Messer Francesco Gualterotti, Giovan Batista Ridolfi, Tommaso Antinori and Piero degli Alberti. When they had so arranged matters that agreement was near, they took the leaders of the friars into the palace and here resolved their difficulties and agreed on terms. But when they were about to start the ordeal, it came to the knowledge of the Franciscans that Fra Domenico was to enter the fire bearing the Host. The began vehemently to reject this proposal, arguing that if the Host were burned it would be a scandal and a grave danger to the whole Christian faith. On the other side Fra Girolamo continued to insist that he should carry it and in the end after much argument, with both sides persisting in their own views and there being no way of reconciling them, they all went home without even lighting the bonfire. And although Fra Girolamo went at once into the pulpit and showed how the failure of the ordeal was due to the Franciscans and that the victory was his many people thought that the question of the Host was quibble rather than a genuine reason; he lost many of his friends that day and public opinion became very hostile to him. In consequence, on the following day his supporters were disillusioned, and were insulted in the streets by the populace, while his adversaries were much emboldened by popular support, and by having the backing of the Compagnacci [a hitherto uncommitted group of young men] under arms and a sympathetic Signoria in the palace. A friar of San Marco was to preach in Santa Liperata after dinner that day, when great tumult arose as if by chance, spreading rapidly throughout the city, as happens when people are excited and minds are full of doubt and suspicion. The enemies of the friar and the Compagnacci took up arms and began to drive the mob toward San Marco. Many of the friar's followers were there at vespers, and they began to defend the convent with weapons and stones although it was not besieged. The fury of the mob then turned toward the house of Francesco Valori, which they attacked while it was defended by those within. Francesco's wife, the daughter of Messer Giovanni Canigiani, appeared at a window and was struck in the head by a spear which killed her instantly. Then the mob broke into the house and found Francesco in an attic; he begged to be taken alive to the palace and was brought outside. As he was accompanied on his way by a guard, he had gone only a few steps when he was attacked and killed by Vincenzo Ridolfi and Simone Tornabuoni in revenge for their kinsmen, Niccolò Ridolfi and Lorenzo Tornabuoni. He was also attacked by Jacopo di Messer Luca Pitti, a violent supporter of the opposite party; but when he struck him he was already dead.

Thus was shown in Francesco Valori a great example of the reversal of fate. But a short time before he had been undoubtedly the city's most important figure in authority, following and popularity: then suddenly all was changed. In the same day his house was sacked, his wife killed before his eyes, and he himself almost at the same moment basely murdered by his enemies; so that many thought God had wished to punish him for having, a few months earlier, refused the right to appeal against their death sentence to Bernardo del Nero and the other citizens of great authority who had long been his friends and colleagues in government. This was a benefit introduced by a new law, and had been allowed to Filippo Corbizzi, Giovanni Benizzi and others, from whom it might have been withheld with more justification considering their relative merits. And so, when circumstances changed, Francesco was killed by their relatives. Yet they, though executed without appeal, had been allowed to state their case and had been condemned by judgment of the magistrates and in a civil way; they had had time at the end to take the sacrament and die like Christians. But Francesco was killed in a skirmish by private hands without being able to utter a word – and in such sharp tumult and sudden calamity that he had no time to recognise, let alone to reflect on, his tragic downfall.

Francesco was a very ambitious and haughty man, so vehement and obstinate in his opinions that he pursued them without scruple, attacking and insulting all who opposed him. On the other hand he was a clever man, and so free of corruption or the taint of taking other men's goods, that there have been few citizens in Florentine politics who can compare with him; and he was greatly and uncompromisingly devoted to the public good. Because of these virtues, added to the nobility of his family and the fact that he was childless, he enjoyed immense popularity for a time; but later his violent manner and his excessively free criticism and sharp words in a free city came to displease the people, and his popularity changed to blame, which made it easier for the friar's enemies and the relatives of the five who had been beheaded to murder him.

When Francesco Valori had been killed and his house sacked, the fury of the mob turned toward the house of Paolantonio Soderini, who after Francesco was with Giovan Batista Ridolfi the leader of that party. However, many men of authority hurried thither who did not hate Paolantonio as they did Francesco, and the Signoria sent guards so that their impetus was checked. If it had not been, it would have resulted in great damage to the city in general, and the ruin of all the leaders of the friar's party in particular. Then the mob returned to San Marco, where a spirited defence was put up, and Jacopo de' Nerli had his eye put out with (I believe) a shot from a crossbow while leading all this disturbance against the friar with a great following of armed youths and disaffected citizens. At last, after many hours of fighting, they forced their way into San Marco and took as prisoners to the palace Fra Girolamo, Fra Domenico, and Fra Silvestro of Florence, who although he did not preach, was one of Fra Girolamo's intimates and was believed to know all his secrets.

When arms had been laid down after this victory, and popular favour and power of government had been transferred to the friar's enemies, they began to concern themselves with consolidating the present state of affairs. As this party did not trust the Ten and the Eight, regarding them as *piagnoni* (which was the name given to the friar's supporters at that time), they summoned the great council and elected a new Eight and Ten, all men trusted by those in power. Doffo Spini, leader of the Compagnacci, was made one of the Eight, and Benedetto de' Nerli, Piero degli Alberti, Piero Popoleschi, Jacopo Pandolfini and other devoted members of that faction were elected to the Ten. Here one should note that although Messer Guido and Bernardo Rucellai were their leaders, and had more authority and following than any others – and had also secretly directed this revolt against the friar's party – neither of them got in when the Ten were elected. In their own districts they were beaten by Giovanni Canacci and Piero Popoleschi. So that, considering how fallacious the judgment of the people is and how much trouble and danger they had undergone without result, they were understandably more determined to save the citizens of the other party – as we shall presently explain.

About twenty citizens were then entrusted with the task of examining Fra Girolamo and his companions – all of them his direst enemies. Eventually, after they had given him a few drops on the *strappado* [instrument of torture], without the Pope's permission, a few days later they drew up a document and published in the great council what they said they had extracted from him. This was signed by the vicars of Florence and Fiesole and by some of the principal friars of San Marco in whose presence the document had been read to Fra Girolamo; and when he was asked if it were true, he agreed that what was written down was true. The most important conclusions were to this effect: the things he had predicted he had not had from God or from revelation or any other divine means – they had been his own invention without the participation or knowledge of any other person lay or cleric; he had acted out of pride and ambition, and his purpose had been to provoke a general council of the Christian princes which should depose the Pope and reform the Church, and if he had been elected Pope he would have accepted; nevertheless he was much more desirous that the great reform should be carried out by his agency than that he should become Pope, because any man may be Pope – even one of little worth – but only a great man could be author and leader of such an endeavour; he had himself planned that to strengthen the government of the city a gonfalonier of justice should be created for life or for a long period, and he thought Francesco Valori more suitable than anyone else – though he disliked his character and overbearing manners. And after him he preferred Giovan Batista Ridolfi, though he disapproved of his high family connections; he had not proposed the ordeal by fire, but Fra Domenico had done so without his knowledge, and he had consented as he could not honourably withdraw and hoping that the Franciscans would be frightened into giving way; and yet he was sure that, if the ordeal were carried out, the Host borne in his friar's hands would save him. These were the conclusions against him; the rest were rather in his favour, for they showed that apart from pride there had been no vice of any kind in him and that he was absolutely innocent of lust, avarice and such sins. And further, that he had not had any political dealings either with princes abroad or citizens within.

When these proceedings had been published, his punishment was delayed for a few days because the Pope having heard of his arrest and his confession, which were most pleasing to him, had sent his absolution not only to the citizens who had examined him without ecclesiastical licence, but to those who had attended his sermons in defiance of the apostolic order. He had then asked that Fra Girolamo should be sent to Rome. This was refused, as it seemed dishonourable that our city should serve as a gaol. In the end he sent the general of the Dominicans and a certain Messer Romolino, a Spaniard whom he later created cardinal, as apostolic commissioners to Florence to examine Fra Girolamo and his companions. While awaiting their arrival, the Florentines began to deal with the case of the citizens who had been his followers. Although no fault could be discovered in them from Fra Girolamo's examination, nor any conspiracy of theirs against the state, nevertheless the voice of the mob was against them. Besides, many wicked citizens who were in the palace and the councils wanted to lay hands on them. Among them was Franceschino degli Albizzi, who, the day Francesco Valori was killed, came to the Signoria and said: 'Your Worships have heard what has happened to Francesco Valori; what do you desire should be done now with Giovan Batista Ridolfi and Paolantonio?' As if to say; if you wish, we will go and kill them. On the other hand Messer Guido, Bernardo Rucellai, the Nerli and those who in fact were the leaders, were strongly in favour of preserving their lives – mainly because, as many thought, they had believed that by overthrowing the friar the great council would be destroyed, and that was why they had worked so vigorously against him. But they were later disillusioned in this, for they saw that many of their followers – the Compagnacci in particular – and all the people wanted to keep the council. So they did not want to lay hands on those citizens without any profit or increase of power, especially as Messer Guido and Bernardo had had the proof in the elections to the Ten of how much reliance they could place on popular favour. It was Bernardo's phrase that all the wrongs in this affair should be taken off the citizens and loaded on the friar. It was therefore decided after some argument and disagreement that they should be spared; although, to satisfy the people, Giovan Batista, Paolantonio and a few other leaders were condemned to make a loan of certain sums of money. In this way the faction was quieted and Giovan Batista and Paolantonio, who had gone away on their friends' advice to allow popular hostility to die down, returned to Florence.

After that the new Signoria was elected with Vieri de' Medici as gonfalonier; and the Signoria included Messer Ormannozzo Deti, Pippo Giugni, Tommasi Gianni and others. During this time the commissioners from Rome arrived, and having re-examined Fra Girolamo and the others, all three were condemned to be burned at the stake. On the 23rd day of May they were first degraded in the Piazza de' Signori, and then hanged and burned before a greater crowd than used to come to their sermons. It was thought an astonishing thing that none of them, particularly Fra Girolamo, should have said anything publicly on that occasion to accuse or excuse themselves.

Thus Girolamo Savonarola came to a shameful end; and perhaps it will not be out of place here to speak at greater length about his qualities, for we have not seen in our times – nor did our fathers and grandfathers in theirs – a monk so full of many virtues or with so much credit and authority as he enjoyed. Even his enemies admit that he was extremely learned in several branches of knowledge, especially philosophy, which he possessed so thoroughly and could use so aptly for all his own purposes as if he had invented it himself – but more particularly in Holy Scripture in which it is believed there had not been anyone to compare with him for several centuries. He had wonderfully sound judgment not only in scholarship but also in worldly affairs, in the principles of which he had great understanding, as in my opinion his sermons show. In this art of preaching he far excelled all others of his time with these qualities of his; for he also possessed an eloquence neither artificial nor forced, but natural and easy. In this he had a quite remarkable reputation and following, for he had preached not only the Lenten sermons but also for many feast days

of the year for so many years on end, in a city full of most subtle
and fastidious minds, where even excellent preachers tend to bore
after a Lenten season or two at most. These qualities of his were so
clear and manifest that his adversaries as well as his supporters and
followers agree in their recognition of them.

[. . .]

When Piero was driven out and the 'parliament' called, the city
was badly shaken and the friends of the former government were
in such disrepute and danger that it seemed impossible to save a
great number of them from violence, Francesco Valori and Piero
Capponi being powerless to defend them. This would have been a
great disaster for the city, as there were among them many good,
wise and rich men of great families and connections. If that had
happened, there would have been violent divisions among those
who ruled the city – as was seen in the example of the Twenty –
and they would have been divided because there were many of
almost equal reputation who desired to be leader; innovations and
'parliaments' would follow, expulsions of citizens, and several
changes of government, and perhaps in the end the violent return
of Piero with infinite destruction and slaughter. Fra Girolamo
alone stopped these tendencies and impulses, introduced the great
council, and so put a bridle on all those with ambitions; he
imposed the appeal to the Signoria, which was a restraint to
preserve the lives of the citizens. He secured universal peace,
which was simply done by removing the opportunity for
punishing the Medici adherents under colour of going back to the
old institutions.

Without any doubt these actions saved Florence; and as he very
truly said, they benefited those who now ruled the city, as well as
those who had ruled in the past. Indeed his works were so good,
while in particular some of his prophecies turned out to be true,
that many have continued for long to believe that he was really
sent by God and a true prophet in spite of the excommunication,
his trial and death. I am doubtful and I have not been able to make
up my mind at all; I must wait – if I live long enough – for time to
reveal the truth. But I draw this conclusion: if he were really a
good man, then we have seen in our days a great prophet; if he
were wicked, then we have seen a great man, because, apart from
his learning, if he were able to feign in public for so many years so

great a mission without ever being caught out in a falsehood, one must admit that he had a most remarkable judgment, talent and power of invention.

With him were executed, as I have said, Fra Domenico and Fra Silvestro, of whom Fra Domenico was a most simple and holy man, such that, if he erred, it was from ingenuousness and not malice. Fra Silvestro was regarded as more astute and more in contact with the townspeople – and yet, according to the trials, unaware of any fraud. But they were killed to satisfy the rage of their enemies, who were commonly called at that time the Arrabbiati.

*Public affairs are easily managed in a city where the body of the people is not corrupt; and where equality exists, there no principality can be established; nor can a republic be established where there is no equality**

Having sufficiently discussed the subject as to what is to be hoped and feared for states that are corrupt, it seems to me not amiss now to examine a resolution of the Senate of Rome in relation to the vow which Camillus had made, to give the tenth part of the booty taken from the Veienti to Apollo. These spoils having fallen into the hands of the Roman people, and there being no other way of having a correct account of it, the Roman Senate issued an edict that every one should bring to the public treasury one tenth part of the booty he had received. And although this decree was not carried into effect, the Senate having devised other ways and means for satisfying Apollo and the people, nevertheless we can see from that resolution how entirely the Senate trusted in the honesty of the people; and how confident they were that no one would fail to return exactly what had been ordered by that edict. And on the other hand we see how the people never for a moment thought of evading it in any way by giving less than what they ought to give, and how they preferred rather to relieve themselves of this imposition by open demonstrations of indignation. This example, together with the many others heretofore cited, proves how much probity and religion these

* *The Historical, Political and Diplomatic Writings of Niccolò Machiavelli*, trans. C. E. Detmold, 4 vols, Boston 1882. Extract from 'Discourses' (I, 55).

people had, and how much good there was to be hoped for from them. And truly, where this probity does not exist, no good is to be expected, as in fact it is vain to look for anything good from those countries which we see nowadays so corrupt, as is the case above all others with Italy. France and Spain also have their share of corruption, and if we do not see so many disorders and troubles in those countries as is the case daily in Italy, it is not so much owing to the goodness of their people, in which they are greatly deficient, as to the fact that they have each a king who keeps them united not only by his virtue, but also by the institutions of those kingdoms, which are as yet preserved pure.

In Germany alone do we see that probity and religion still exist largely amongst the people, in consequence of which many republics exist there in the full enjoyment of liberty, observing their laws in such manner that no one from within or without could venture upon an attempt to master them. And in proof that the ancient virtue still prevails there in great part, I will cite an example similar to that given above of the Senate and people of Rome. When these republics have occasion to spend any considerable amount of money for public account, their magistrates or councils, who have authority in these matters, impose upon all the inhabitants a tax of one or two per cent of their possessions. When such a resolution has been passed according to the laws of the country, every citizen presents himself before the collectors of this impost, and after having taken an oath to pay the just amount, deposits in a strong-box provided for the purpose the sum which according to his conscience he ought to pay, without any one's witnessing what he pays. From this we may judge of the extent of the probity and religion that still exist amongst those people. And we must presume that every one pays the true amount, for if this were not the case the impost would not yield the amount intended according to the estimates based upon former impositions; the fraud would thus be discovered, and other means would be employed to collect the amount required. This honesty is the more to be admired as it is so very rare that it is found only in that country; and this results from two causes. The one is, that the Germans have no great commerce with their neighbours, few strangers coming amongst them, and they rarely visiting foreign countries, but being content to remain at home and to live on what their country produces, and to clothe themselves with the wool from their own flocks, which takes away all occasion for intimate intercourse with strangers and all opportunity of corruption. Thus they have been prevented from adopting either French, Spanish or Italian customs, and these nations are the great corrupters of the world. The other cause is, that those republics which have thus preserved their political existence uncorrupted do not permit any of their citizens to be or to live in the manner of gentlemen, but rather maintain amongst them a perfect equality, and are the most decided enemies of the lords and gentlemen that exist in the country; so that if by chance any of them fall into their hands, they kill them, as being the chief promoters of all corruption and troubles.

And to explain more clearly what is meant by the term gentlemen, I say that those are called gentlemen who live idly upon the proceeds of their extensive possessions, without devoting themselves to agriculture or any other useful pursuit to gain a living. Such men are pernicious to any country or republic, but more pernicious even than these are such as have, besides their other possessions, castles which they command, and subjects who obey them. This class of men abound in the kingdom of Naples, in the Roman territory, in the Romagna, in Lombardy; whence it is that no republic has ever been able to exist in those countries, nor have they been able to preserve any regular political existence, for that class of men are everywhere enemies of all civil government. And to attempt the establishment of a republic in a country so constituted would be impossible. The only way to establish any kind of order there is to found a monarchical government; for where the body of the people is so thoroughly corrupt that the laws are powerless for restraint, it becomes necessary to establish some superior power which with a royal hand, and with full and absolute powers, may put a curb upon the excessive ambition and corruption of the powerful. This is verified by the example of Tuscany, where in a comparatively small extent of territory there have for a long time existed three republics, Florence, Siena and Lucca; and although the other cities of this territory are in a measure subject to these, yet we see that in spirit and by their institutions they maintain, or attempt to maintain, their liberty; all of which is due to the fact that there are in that country no lords possessing castles, and exceedingly few or no gentlemen. On the contrary, there is such a general equality that it would be easy for any man of sagacity, well versed in the ancient forms of civil government, to introduce a republic there; but the misfortunes of that country have been so great that up to the present time no man has arisen who has had the power and ability to do so.

We may then draw the following conclusion from what has been said: that if any one should wish to establish a republic in a country where there are many gentlemen, he will not succeed until he has destroyed them all; and whoever desires to establish a kingdom or principality where liberty and equality prevail, will equally fail, unless he withdraws from that general equality a number of the boldest and most ambitious spirits, and makes gentlemen of them, not merely in name but in fact, by giving to them castles and possessions, as well as money and subjects; so that surrounded by these he may be able to maintain his power, and that by his support they may satisfy their ambition, and the others may be constrained to submit to that yoke to which force alone has been able to subject them. And as in this way definite relations will be established between the ruler and his subjects, they will be maintained in their respective ranks. But to establish a republic in a country better adapted to a monarchy, or a monarchy where a republic would be more suitable, requires a man of rare genius and power, and therefore out of the many that have attempted it but few have succeeded; for the greatness of the enterprise frightens men so that they fail even in the very beginning. Perhaps the opinion which I have expressed, that a republic cannot be established where there are gentlemen, may seem to be contradicted by the experience of the Venetian republic, in which none but gentlemen could attain to any rank or public employment. And yet this example is in no way opposed to my theory, for the gentlemen of Venice are so more in name than in fact; for they have no great revenues from estates, their riches being founded upon commerce and a movable property, and moreover none of them have castles or jurisdiction over subjects, but the name of gentleman is only a title of dignity and respect, and is in no way based upon the things that gentlemen enjoy in other countries. And as all other republics have different classes under different names, so Venice is divided into gentlemen and commonalty, and the former have all the offices and honours, from which the latter are entirely excluded; and this distribution causes no disorders in that republic, for the reasons elsewhere given. Let republics, then, be established where equality exists, and, on the contrary, principalities where great inequality prevails; otherwise the governments will lack proper proportions and have but little durability.

What nations the Romans had to contend against, and with what obstinacy they defended their liberty*

Nothing required so much effort on the part of the Romans to subdue the nations around them, as well as those of more distant countries, as the love of liberty which these people cherished in those days; and which they defended with so much obstinacy, that nothing but the exceeding valour of the Romans could ever have subjugated them. For we know from many instances to what danger they exposed themselves to preserve or recover their liberty, and what vengeance they practised upon those who had deprived them of it. The lessons of history teach us also, on the other hand, the injuries people suffer from servitude. And whilst in our own times there is only one country in which we can say that free communities exist, in those ancient times all countries contained numerous cities that enjoyed entire liberty. In the times of which we are now speaking, there were in Italy from the mountains that divide the present Tuscany from Lombardy, down to the extreme point, a number of independent nations, such as the Tuscans, the Romans, the Samnites and many others, that inhabited the rest of Italy. Nor is there ever any mention of there having been other kings besides those that reigned in Rome, and Porsenna, king of the Tuscans, whose line became extinct in a manner not mentioned in history. But we do see that, at the time when the Romans went to besiege Veii, Tuscany was

* The Historical, Political and Diplomatic Writings of Niccolò Machiavelli, trans. C. E. Detmold, 4 vols, Boston 1882. Extract from 'Discourses' (II, 2).

free, and so prized her liberty and hated the very name of king, that when the Veienti had created a king in their city for its defence, and applied to the Tuscans for help against the Romans, it was resolved, after repeated deliberations, not to grant such assistance to the Veienti so long as they lived under that king; for the Tuscans deemed it not well to engage in the defence of those who had voluntarily subjected themselves to the rule of one man. And it is easy to understand whence that affection for liberty arose in the people, for they had seen that cities never increased in dominion or wealth unless they were free. And certainly it is wonderful to think of the greatness which Athens attained within the space of a hundred years after having freed herself from the tyranny of Pisistratus; and still more wonderful is it to reflect upon the greatness which Rome achieved after she was rid of her kings. The cause of this is manifest, for it is not individual prosperity, but the general good, that makes cities great; and certainly the general good is regarded nowhere but in republics, because whatever they do is for the common benefit, and should it happen to prove an injury to one or more individuals, those for whose benefit the thing is done are so numerous that they can always carry the measure against the few that are injured by it. But the very reverse happens where there is a prince whose private interests are generally in opposition to those of the city, whilst the measures taken for the benefit of the city are seldom deemed personally advantageous by the prince. This state of things soon leads to a tyranny, the least evil of which is to check the advance of the city in its career of prosperity, so that it grows neither in power nor wealth, but on the contrary rather retrogrades. And if fate should have it that the tyrant is enterprising, and by his courage and valour extends his dominions, it will never be for the benefit of the city, but only for his own; for he will never bestow honours and office upon the good and brave citizens over whom he tyrannises, so that he may not have occasion to suspect and fear them. Nor will he make the states which he conquers subject or tributary to the city of which he is the despot, because it would not be to his advantage to make that city powerful, but it will always be for his interest to keep the state disunited, so that each place and country shall recognise him only as master; thus he alone, and not his country, profits by his conquests. Those who desire to have this opinion confirmed by many other arguments, need but read Xenophon's treatise *On Tyranny*.

It is no wonder, then, that the ancients hated tyranny and loved freedom, and that the very name of liberty should have been held in such esteem by them; as was shown by the Syracusans when Hieronymus, the nephew of Hiero, was killed. When his death became known to his army, which was near Syracuse, it caused at first some disturbances, and they were about committing violence upon his murderers; but when they learnt that the cry of liberty had been raised in Syracuse, they were delighted, and instantly returned to order. Their fury against the tyrannicides was quelled, and they thought only of how a free government might be established in Syracuse. Nor can we wonder that the people indulge in extraordinary revenge against those who have robbed them of their liberty; of which we could cite many instances; but will quote only one that occurred in Corcyra, a city in Greece, during the Peloponnesian war. Greece was at that time divided into two parties, one of which adhered to the Athenians, and the other to the Spartans, and a similar division of parties existed in most of the Greek cities. It happened that in Corcyra the nobles, being the stronger party, seized upon the liberties of the people; but with the assistance of the Athenians the popular party recovered its power, and having seized the nobles, they tied their hands behind their backs, and threw them into a prison large enough to hold them all. They thence took eight or ten at a time, under pretence of sending them into exile in different directions; but instead of that they killed them with many cruelties. When the remainder became aware of this, they resolved if possible to escape such an ignominious death; and having armed themselves as well as they could, they resisted those who attempted to enter the prison; but when the people heard this disturbance, they pulled down the roof and upper portion of the prison, and suffocated the nobles within under its ruins. Many such notable and horrible cases occurred in that country, which shows that the people will avenge their lost liberty with more energy than when it is merely threatened.

Reflecting now as to whence it came that in ancient times the people were more devoted to liberty than in the present, I believe that it resulted from this, that men were stronger in those days, which I believe to be attributable to the difference of education, founded upon the difference of their religion and ours. For as our religion teaches us the truth and the true way of life, it causes us to attach less value to the honours and possessions of this world; whilst the pagans, esteeming those things as the highest good, were more energetic and ferocious in their actions. We may observe this also in most of their institutions, beginning with the magnificence of their sacrifices as compared with the humility of ours, which are gentle solemnities rather than magnificent ones, and have nothing of energy or ferocity in them, whilst in theirs there was no lack of pomp and show, to which was superadded the ferocious and bloody nature of the sacrifice by the slaughter of many animals; and the familiarity with this terrible sight assimilated the nature of men to their sacrificial ceremonies. Besides, this, the pagan religion deified only men who had achieved great glory, such as commanders of armies and chiefs or republics, whilst ours glorifies more the humble and contemplative men than the men of action. Our religion, moreover, places the supreme happiness in humility, lowliness and a contempt for worldly objects, whilst the other, on the contrary, places the supreme good in grandeur of soul, strength of body, and all such other qualities as render men formidable; and if our religion claims of us fortitude of soul, it is more to enable us to suffer than to achieve great deeds.

These principles seem to me to have made men feeble, and caused them to become an easy prey to evil-minded men, who can control them more securely, seeing that the great body of men, for the sake of gaining Paradise, are more disposed to endure injuries than to avenge them. And although it would seem that the world has become effeminate and Heaven disarmed, yet this arises unquestionably from the baseness of men, who have interpreted our religion according to the promptings of indolence rather than those of virtue. For if we were to reflect that our religion permits us to exalt and defend our country, we should see that according to it we ought also to love and honour our country, and prepare ourselves so as to be capable of defending her. It is this education, then, and this false interpretation of our religion, that is the cause of there not being so many republics nowadays as there were anciently; and that there is no longer the same love of liberty amongst the people now as there was then. I believe, however, that another reason for this will be found in the fact that the Roman Empire, by force of arms, destroyed all the republics and free cities; and although that empire was afterwards itself dissolved, yet these cities could not reunite themselves nor reorganise their civil institutions, except in a very few instances.

*To found a new republic, or to reform entirely the old institutions of an existing one, must be the work of one man only**

It may perhaps appear to some that I have gone too far into the details of Roman history before having made any mention of the founders of that republic, or of her institutions, her religion and her military establishment. Not wishing, therefore, to keep any longer in suspense the desires of those who wish to understand these matters, I say that many will perhaps consider it an evil example that the founder of a civil society, as Romulus was, should first have killed his brother, and then have consented to the death of Titus Tatius, who had been elected to share the royal authority with him; from which it might be concluded that the citizens, according to the example of their prince, might, from ambition and the desire to rule, destroy those who attempt to oppose their authority. This opinion would be correct, if we do not take into consideration the object which Romulus had in view in committing that homicide. But we must assume, as a general rule, that it never or rarely happens that a republic or monarchy is well constituted, or its old institutions entirely reformed, unless it is done by only one individual; it is even necessary that he whose mind has conceived such a constitution should be alone in carrying it into effect. A sagacious legislator of a republic, therefore, whose object is to promote the public good, and not his private interests, and who prefers his country to his

* *The Historical, Political and Diplomatic Writings of Niccolò Machiavelli*, trans. C. E. Detmold, 4 vols, Boston 1882. Extract from 'Discourses', (I, 9).

own successors, should concentrate all authority in himself; and a wise mind will never censure any one for having employed any extraordinary means for the purpose of establishing a kingdom or constituting a republic. It is well that, when the act accuses him, the result should excuse him; and when the result is good, as in the case of Romulus, it will always absolve him from blame. For he is to be reprehended who commits violence for the purpose of destroying, and not he who employs it for beneficent purposes. The lawgiver should, however, be sufficiently wise and virtuous not to leave this authority which he has assumed either to his heirs or to any one else; for mankind being more prone to evil than to good, his successor might employ for evil purposes the power which he had used only for good ends. Besides, although one man alone should organise a government, yet it will not endure long if the administration of it remains on the shoulders of a single individual; it is well, then, to confide this to the charge of many, for thus it will be sustained by the many. Therefore, as the organisation of anything cannot be made by many, because the divergence of their opinions hinders them from agreeing as to what is best, yet, when once they do understand it, they will not readily agree to abandon it. That Romulus deserves to be excused for the death of his brother and that of his associate, and that what he had done was for the general good, and not for the gratification of his own ambition, is proved by the fact that he immediately instituted a senate with which to consult, and according to the opinions of which he might form his resolutions. And on carefully considering the authority which Romulus reserved for himself, we see that all he kept was the command of the army in case of war, and the power of convoking the senate. This was seen when Rome became free, after the expulsion of the Tarquins, when there was no other innovation made upon the existing order of things than the substitution of two consuls, appointed annually, in place of an hereditary king; which proves clearly that all the original institutions of that city were more in conformity with the requirements of a free and civil society than with an absolute and tyrannical government.

The above views might be corroborated by any number of examples, such as those of Moses, Lycurgus, Solon, and other founders of monarchies and republics, who were enabled to establish laws suitable for the general good only by keeping for themselves an exclusive authority; but all these are so well known that I will not further refer to them. I will adduce only one instance, not so celebrated, but which merits the consideration of those who aim to become good legislators: it is this. Agis, king of Sparta, desired to bring back the Spartans to the strict observance of the laws of Lycurgus, being convinced that, by deviating from them, their city had lost much of her ancient virtue, and consequently her power and dominion; but the Spartan ephors had him promptly killed, as one who attempted to make himself a tyrant. His successor, Cleomenes, had conceived the same desire, from studying the records and writings of Agis, which he had found, and which explained his aims and intentions. Cleomenes was convinced that he would be unable to render this service to his country unless he possessed sole authority; for he judged that, owing to the ambitious nature of men, he could not promote the interests of the many against the will of the few; and therefore he availed himself of a convenient opportunity to have all the ephors slain, as well as all such others as might oppose his project, after which he restored the laws of Lycurgus entirely. This course was calculated to resuscitate the greatness of Sparta, and to give Cleomenes a reputation equal to that of Lycurgus, had it not been for the power of the Macedonians and the weakness of the other Greek republics. For being soon after attacked by the Macedonians, and Sparta by herself being inferior in strength, and there being no one whom he could call to his aid, he was defeated; and thus his project, so just and laudable, was never put into execution. Considering, then, all these things, I conclude that, to found a republic, one must be alone; and that Romulus deserves to be absolved from, and not blamed for, the death of Remus and of Tatius.

To Francesco Vettori, his benefactor*

10 December 1513, Florence

MAGNIFICENT AMBASSADOR – 'Never late were favours divine.' [Petrarch] I say this because I seemed to have lost – no, rather mislaid – your good will; you had not written to me for a long time, and I was wondering what the reason could be. And of all those that came into my mind I took little account, except of one only, when I feared that you had stopped writing because somebody had written to you that I was not a good guardian of your letters, and I knew that, except Filippo and Pagolo, nobody by my doing had seen them. I have found it again through your last letter of the twenty-third of the past month, from which I learn with pleasure how regularly and quietly you carry on this public office, and I encourage you to continue so, because he who gives up his own convenience for the convenience of others, only loses his own and from them gets no gratitude. And since fortune wants to do everything, she wishes us to let her do it, to be quiet, and not to give her trouble, and to wait for a time when she will allow something to be done by men; and then will be the time for you to work harder, to stir things up more, and for me to leave my farm and say: 'Here I am.' I cannot however, wishing to return equal favours, tell you in this letter anything else than what my life is; and if you judge that you would like to swap with me, I shall be glad to.

I am living on my farm, and since I had my last bad luck, I have not spent twenty days, putting them all together, in Florence. I

---

* N. Machiavelli, *The Letters of Machiavelli: A Selection*, ed. and trans. by A. Gilbert, Capricorn Books, New York 1961. Letter 137.

have until now been snaring thrushes with my own hands. I got up before day, prepared birdlime, went out with a bundle of cages on my back, so that I looked like Geta when he was returning from the harbour with Amphitryon's books [reference to a story in Plautus]. I caught at least two thrushes and at most six. And so I did all September. Then this pastime, pitiful and strange as it is, gave out, to my displeasure. And of what sort my life is, I shall tell you.

I get up in the morning with the sun and go into a grove I am having cut down, where I remain two hours to look over the work of the past day and kill some time with the cutters, who have always some bad-luck story ready, about either themselves or their neighbours. And as to this grove I could tell you a thousand fine things that have happened to me, in dealing with Frosino da Panzano and others who wanted some of this firewood. And Frosino especially sent for a number of cords [a measurement of wood] without saying a thing to me, and on payment he wanted to keep back from me ten lire, which he says he should have had from me four years ago, when he beat me at *cricca* at Antonio Guicciardini's. I raised the devil, and was going to prosecute as a thief the waggoner who came for the wood, but Giovanni Machiavelli came between us and got us to agree. Batista Guicciardini, Filippo Ginori, Tommaso del Bene and some other citizens, when that north wind was blowing, each ordered a cord from me. I made promises to all and sent one to Tommaso, which at Florence changed to half a cord, because it was piled up again by himself, his wife, his servant, his children, so that he looked like Gabburra when on Thursday with all his servants he cudgels an ox. Hence, having seen for whom there was profit, I told the others I had no more wood, and all of them were angry about it, and especially Batista, who counts this along with his misfortunes at Prato. [He was in command there when it was taken by the Spanish in 1512.]

Leaving the grove, I go to a spring, and thence to my aviary. I have a book in my pocket, either Dante or Petrarch, or one of the lesser poets, such as Tibullus, Ovid and the like. I read of their tender passions and their loves, remember mine, enjoy myself a while in that sort of dreaming. Then I move along the road to the inn; I speak with those who pass, ask news of their villages, learn various things, and note the various tastes and different fancies of men. In the course of these things comes the hour for dinner, where with my family I eat such food as this poor farm of mine and my tiny property allow. Having eaten, I go back to the inn; there is the host, usually a butcher, a miller, two furnace tenders. With these I sink into vulgarity for the whole day, playing at *cricca* and at trich-trach, and then these games bring on a thousand disputes and countless insults with offensive words, and usually we are fighting over a penny, and nevertheless we are heard shouting as far as San Casciano. So, involved in these trifles, I keep my brain from growing mouldy, and satisfy the malice of this fate of mine, being glad to have her drive me along this road, to see if she will be ashamed of it.

On the coming of evening, I return to my house and enter my study; and at the door I take off the day's clothing, covered with mud and dust, and put on garments regal and courtly; and reclothed appropriately, I enter the ancient courts of ancient men, where, received by them with affection, I feed on that food which only is mine and which I was born for, where I am not ashamed to speak with them and to ask them the reason for their actions; and they in their kindness answer me; and for four hours of time I do not feel boredom, I forget every trouble, I do not dread poverty, I am not frightened by death; entirely I give myself over to them.

And because Dante says it does not produce knowledge when we hear but do not remember, I have noted everything in their conversation which has profited me, and have composed a little work *On Princedoms*, where I go as deeply as I can into considerations on this subject, debating what a princedom is, of what kinds they are, how they are gained, how they are kept, why they are lost. And if ever you can find any of my fantasies pleasing, this one should not displease you; and by a prince, and especially by a new prince, it ought to be welcomed. Hence I am dedicating it to His Magnificence Giuliano. Filippo Casavecchia has seen it; he can give you some account in part of the thing in itself and of the discussions I have had with him, though I am still enlarging and revising it.

You wish, Magnificent Ambassador, that I leave this life and come to enjoy yours with you. I shall do it in any case, but what tempts me now are certain affairs that within six weeks I shall finish. What makes me doubtful is that the Soderini we know so well are in the city, whom I should be obliged, on coming there, to visit and talk with. I should fear that on my return I could not hope to dismount at my house but should dismount at the prison, because though this government has mighty foundations and great security, yet it is new and therefore suspicious, and there is no lack of wiseacres who, to make a figure, like Pagolo Bertini, would place others at the dinner table and leave the reckoning to me. I beg you to rid me of this fear, and then I shall come within the time mentioned to visit you in any case.

I have talked with Filippo about this little work of mine that I have spoken of, whether it is good to give it or not to give it; and if it is good to give it, whether it would be good to take it myself, or whether I should send it there. Not giving it would make me fear that at the least Giuliano will not read it and that this rascal Ardinghelli [Secretary to Pope Leo X] will get himself honour from this latest work of mine. The giving of it is forced on me by the necessity that drives me, because I am using up my money, and I cannot remain as I am a long time without becoming despised through poverty. In addition, there is my wish that our present Medici lords will make use of me, even if they begin by making me roll a stone; because then if I could not gain their favour, I should complain of myself; and through this thing, if it were read, they would see that for the fifteen years while I have been studying the art of the state, I have not slept or been playing; and well may anybody be glad to get the services of one who at the expense of others has become full of experience. And of my honesty there should be no doubt, because having always preserved my honesty, I shall hardly now learn to break it; and he who has been honest and good for forty-three years, as I have, cannot change his nature; and as a witness to my honesty and goodness I have my poverty.

I should like, then, to have you also write me what you think best on this matter, and I give you my regards. Be happy.

Niccolò Machiavelli

The Art of War*

[Fabrizio and his audience]

When Fabrizio Colonna returned from Lombardy, where he had long been campaigning for the Catholic king with great glory to himself, he decided, as he was passing through Florence, to rest some days in that city in order to visit His Excellency the Duke and to see again some gentlemen with whom in the past he had been acquainted. Hence Cosimo thought it proper to invite him to a banquet in his gardens [Oricellari], not so much to exercise his own liberality as to have a reason for speaking with him at length, and from him hearing and learning various things such as from a man of that sort can be hoped for, since it seemed to Cosimo a chance to spend a day in talking about those matters that brought satisfaction to his own spirit. So Fabrizio came as Cosimo wished and was received by him along with other faithful friends, among whom were Zanobi Buondelmonti, Batista della Palla and Luigi Alamanni, all young men loved by him and zealous in the same studies, whose good qualities, because every day and every hour they are their own praise, we shall omit. Fabrizio, then, according to the times and the place, was by all of them honoured with the greatest possible honours.

[The ancients to be imitated in vigour]

But when the pleasures of the banquet were over, and the tables were cleared and every sort of festivity had been concluded – something that in the presence of noble men whose minds are

* N. Machiavelli, *The Chief Works and Others*, trans. A. Gilbert, Duke University Press, North Carolina 1965. Extract from 'The Art of War', Vol. 2, Book 1.

intent on honourable thoughts is concluded quickly – since the day was long and the heat great, Cosimo thought that in order better to satisfy his desire it would be well, using the excuse of escaping the heat, to go to the most secluded and shady part of his garden. When they had arrived there and taken seats, some on the grass, which is very fresh in that place, some on the seats arranged in those spots under the shade of very tall trees, Fabrizio praised the spot as delightful, and observing the trees closely and failing to recognise some of them, he was puzzled. Observing this, Cosimo said: 'You perhaps do not know some of these trees; but do not think it strange, because some of them were more renowned by the ancients than today they are by common custom.' And having told him their names and how Bernardo his grandfather had busied himself with such cultivation, he was answered by Fabrizio: 'I was thinking that it might be as you say, and this place and this avocation were making me remember some princes of the kingdom, to whom these ancient plantings and shades give pleasure.' And pausing in his remarks at this point and sitting for a while as though inwardly intent on something, he added: 'If I thought I should not give offence, I would tell you my opinion of it, but I do not believe I shall offend, since I am speaking with friends, and in order to discuss things and not in order to censure them. How much better they would have done (be it said with due respect to all) to seek to be like the ancients in things strong and rough, not in those delicate and soft, and in those that are done in the sun, not in the shade, and to take their methods from an antiquity that is true and perfect, not from that which is false and corrupt, because as soon as activities of this sort satisfied my Romans, my native land went to ruin.' To which Cosimo replied – but to escape the bother of having to repeat so many times *He said* and *The other answered*, I shall give only the name of him who speaks, without repeating anything else. So then said

[Men imitating antiquity would be thought peculiar]

COSIMO: You have opened the way to a discussion that I was wishing for, and I pray you to speak without reservation, because without reservation I shall question you. And if in asking or replying I excuse or accuse anybody, it will not be for the sake of excuse or accusation but to learn from you the truth.

FABRIZIO: And I shall be very glad to tell you what I understand of all you ask; as to whether it be true or not, I shall resign myself to your judgment. And to me it will be pleasant to have you ask, because I am just as ready to learn from you when you ask as you are from me when I answer, because many times a wise questioner makes one consider many things and come to know many others which, if one had not been asked about, one would never have known.

COSIMO: I wish to turn to what you said first, that my grandfather and those princes of yours would have been wiser to imitate the ancients in things harsh rather than in those delicate; but I wish to offer excuse for my side, because I shall leave the excusing of the other to you. I do not believe there was, in his times, any man who so much detested soft living as he did and was such a lover of that severe life you praise. Yet he realised that neither in his own person nor in those of his children could he follow it, because he was born in an age so corrupt, in which one who wished to depart from the usual habit would be defamed and spoken against by everybody. Because if a naked man, in the summer, under the midday sun should stretch out on the sand, or in the winter in the coldest months on the snow, as Diogenes did, he would be thought crazy. If anyone, like the Spartans, should bring up his children in the country, should make them sleep in the open air, go with their heads and their feet bare, bathe in cold water, in order to bring them to be able to bear distress and to make them have less affection for life and less fear of death, he would be mocked and held to be rather an animal than a man. If anyone also fed on vegetables and despised gold, like Fabricius, he would be praised by few and followed by none. Hence, dismayed by our methods of living at present, he abandoned the ancients, yet whenever he could without causing great astonishment imitate antiquity, he did so.

[*The Romans to be imitated in public affairs*]

FABRIZIO: You have excused him in this matter with great vigour, and certainly you speak the truth. But I was not referring so much to those severe methods of living as to other methods, more humane and more in harmony with the life of today, which I do not believe that one counted among the leading men of a city would find it difficult to introduce. I shall never depart, in giving examples of anything, from my Romans. If we consider their life and the organisation of their republic, we shall see there many things not impossible for introduction into any state in which there is still left something good.

COSIMO: What are these things you would like to introduce that are like the ancient ones?

FABRIZIO: To honour and reward excellence, not to despise poverty, to esteem the methods and regulations of military discipline, to oblige the citizens to love one another, to live without factions, to esteem private less than public good, and other like things that could easily fit in with our times. About these customs, it is not difficult to be persuaded when one thinks about them enough and takes them up in the right way, because in them so plainly can be seen the truth that every public-spirited nature is capable of receiving. He who accomplishes such a thing plants trees beneath the shade of which mankind lives more prosperously and more happily than beneath this shade.

COSIMO: I do not intend to reply to what you have said in any way, but I wish to let the decision about it be turned over to those who easily can judge it; and I shall direct my speech to you who blame those who in serious and great actions do not imitate the ancients, believing that in this way my intention will be more easily fulfilled. I should like, then, to learn from you why it is that on one side you condemn those who in their acts do not imitate the ancients, and that on the other, in war, which is your profession and in which you are considered excellent, we do not see that you have used any ancient methods, or any showing some likeness to them.

[Ancient example for warfare]

FABRIZIO: You have appeared just where I expected you, because my speech did not deserve any other question, nor was there any other that I desired. And though I might acquit myself with an easy excuse, nevertheless, for my own greater satisfaction and yours, since the time is propitious, I wish to enter into a longer discussion. Men who wish to do anything ought first with all diligence to make preparations, in order that when an occasion comes, they may be ready to carry out what they have intended beforehand to do. And because when preparations are made cautiously they are not known about, no man can be accused of any negligence, if his plan is not revealed before that occasion. But when it comes, if nothing is done, he appears as not having prepared himself enough to be adequate or as in some respect not having made decisions. Because no occasion has come to me for showing the preparations I have made for bringing the soldiers back into their ancient courses, if I have not brought them back, neither by you nor by others can I be censured. I believe this excuse enough for a reply to your accusation.

COSIMO: It would be enough, if I were sure the occasion had not come.

FABRIZIO: But because I know that you can doubt whether this occasion has come or not, I intend, if you are willing patiently to listen, to discuss at length what sort of preparations must be made beforehand, what sort of occasion has to arise, what sort of difficulty keeps the preparations from being effective and the occasion from coming, and how this thing at the same instant, though the terms seem contrary, is very difficult and very easy to do.

COSIMO: You cannot do, both for me and for these others, a thing more pleasing than this, and if it is not irksome for you to speak, never will it be irksome for us to hear. But because this discourse must be long, I want aid from these friends of mine, with your permission; and they and I beg from you one thing: that you will not be annoyed if sometimes we interrupt you with some urgent question.

FABRIZIO: I am very willing that you, Cosimo, and these other young men should here question me, because I believe that your youth makes you more interested in military matters and readier to believe what I shall say. Men of another age, with their hair white and the blood in their bodies turned to ice, are commonly some of them enemies of war, some beyond correction, believing that the times and not bad customs force men to live thus. So ask questions of me, all of you, with assurance and without hesitation; this I wish both because it will give me a little rest and because I shall be glad not to leave in your minds any uncertainty.

[*Professional soldiers cannot be good men*]

I wish to begin with your words, in which you said to me that in war, which is my profession, I have not used any ancient methods. On this I say that because this is a profession by means of which men cannot live virtuously at all times, it cannot be practised as a profession except by a republic or a kingdom; and neither of these, when they have been well regulated, has ever allowed one of its citizens or subjects to practise it as a profession, nor has any good man ever engaged in it as his special profession. Because he will never be reckoned a good man who carries on an occupation in which, if he is to endeavour at all times to get income from it, he must be rapacious, fraudulent, violent, and must have many qualities which of necessity make him not good; nor can men who practise it as a profession, the big as well as the little, be of any other sort, because this profession does not support them in time of peace. Hence they are obliged either to hope that there will be no peace, or to become so rich in time of war that in peace they can support themselves. And neither one of these two expectations is to be found in a good man, because from the desire to support themselves at all times come the robberies, the deeds of violence, the murderous acts that such soldiers commit as much against their friends as against their enemies; and from not wishing peace come the deceits that the generals practise against those by whom they are employed, in order that a war may last; and if peace does come, it often happens that the generals, being deprived of their stipends and of their living, lawlessly set up their ensigns as soldiers of fortune and without any mercy plunder a region.

APPENDIX E

*History of Florence**

After the successful termination of the war of Serezana, the Florentines lived in prosperous tranquillity until the death of Lorenzo de' Medici in 1492; for after having established peace by his good judgment and authority, Lorenzo devoted his attention to the aggrandisement of the city and of his own family. He married his eldest son Piero to Alfonsina, daughter of the Cavaliere Orsini, and had his second son promoted to the dignity of cardinal, which was the more remarkable as it was unprecedented, the youth having hardly completed his thirteenth year. This was in fact a ladder by means of which his house was enabled to mount to heaven itself, as indeed it happened in the course of time. He could not provide equally good fortune for his third son, as he was still too young when Lorenzo died. Of his daughters, one was married to Jacopo Salviati, another to Francesco Cibo, and a third to Piero Ridolfi; but the fourth, who, by way of keeping the family united, had been married to Giovanni de' Medici, her cousin, died. In his commercial affairs, however, Lorenzo was very unfortunate; for through the irregularity of his agents, who managed his affairs, not like those of a private individual, but of a prince, the greater part of his private fortune was consumed; so that he was obliged to call upon his country to aid him with large sums of money. In consequence of this he gave up all commercial operations, and turned his attention to landed property, as being a more safe and solid wealth. He acquired large possessions in the

* *The Historical, Political and Diplomatic Writings of Niccolò Machiavelli*, trans. C. E. Detmold, 4 vols, Boston 1882. Extract from 'The History of Florence', Vol. 1, Book 8, 36.

districts of Prato and Pisa, and in the Val di Pesa, and erected upon them useful and elegant buildings, not like a private citizen, but with truly royal magnificence. After that he directed his attention to extending and embellishing the city of Florence, in which there was still much vacant land. Here he had new streets laid out and built up with houses, whereby the city was greatly enlarged and beautified. And to secure greater quiet and security within the state, and to be able to resist and combat its enemies at a greater distance from the city, he fortified the castle of Firenzuola, in the mountains towards Bologna; in the direction of Siena he began the restoration of the Poggio Imperiale, which he fortified in the most complete manner. Towards Genoa he closed the road to the enemy by the acquisition of Pietrasanta and Serezana. Besides this, he maintained his friends the Baglioni in Perugia with subsidies and pensions, and the same with the Vitelli in Città di Castello; and in Faenza he kept a special governor; all of which measures served as strong bulwarks to the city of Florence.

In peaceful times he often entertained the people with various festivities, such as jousts, feats of arms, and representations of triumphs of olden times. He aimed to maintain abundance in the city, to keep the people united and the nobility honoured. He had the greatest love and admiration for all who excelled in any art, and was a great patron of learning and of literary men, of which his conduct towards Cristofano Landini and Messer Demetrius the Greek furnishes the strongest proof. For this reason the Count Giovanni della Mirandola, a man of almost supernatural genius, was attracted by the magnificence of Lorenzo, and preferred to establish his home in Florence rather than in any other part of Europe, all of which he had visited in his travels. Lorenzo took the greatest delight in architecture, music and poetry; and many of his own poetic compositions, enriched with commentaries, appeared in print. And for the purpose of enabling the Florentine youths to devote themselves to the study of letters, he established a university in the city of Pisa, where he employed the most eminent men of all Italy as professors. He built a monastery for Fra Mariano da Chianozzona, of the order of St Augustine, who was a most admirable pulpit orator. And thus, beloved of God and fortune, all his enterprises were crowned with success, whilst those of his enemies had the opposite fate. For besides the conspiracy of the Pazzi, Battista Frescobaldi also attempted his assassination in the church of the Carmine; and Baldinatto of Pistoia tried the same at his villa. Each of these, together with their accomplices, suffered the most just punishment for their nefarious attempts.

Thus Lorenzo's mode of life, his ability and good fortune, were recognised with admiration, and highly esteemed, not only by all the princes of Italy, but also by those at a great distance. Matthias, King of Hungary, gave him many proofs of his affection; the Sultan of Egypt sent ambassadors to him with precious gifts; and the Grand Turk gave up to him Bernardo Bandini, the murderer of his brother. These proofs of regard from foreign sovereigns caused Lorenzo to be looked upon with the greatest admiration by all Italy; and his reputation was daily increased by his rare ability, for he was eloquent and subtle in speech, wise in his resolves, and bold and prompt in their execution. Nor can he be charged with any vices that would stain his many virtues, though very fond of women, and delighting in the society of witty and sarcastic men, and even taking pleasure in puerile amusements – more so than would seem becoming to so great a man, so that he was often seen taking part in the childish sports of his sons and daughters. Considering, then, his fondness for pleasure, and at the same time his grave character, there seemed as it were united in him two almost incompatible natures. During his latter years he was greatly afflicted with sufferings from his malady, the gout, and oppressed with intolerable pains in his stomach, which increased to that degree that he died in the month of April, 1492, in the forty-fourth year of his age. Neither Florence nor all Italy ever lost a man of higher reputation for prudence and ability, or whose loss was more deplored by his country, than Lorenzo de' Medici. And as his death was to be followed by the most ruinous consequences, Heaven gave many manifest indications of it. Amongst these was that the highest pinnacle of the church of the Santa Reparata was struck by lightning, so that a large part of the pinnacle fell to the earth, filling every one with terror and amazement. All Florence, then, as well as all the princes of Italy, lamented the death of Lorenzo; in proof of which there was not one who did not send ambassadors to Florence to express his grief at so great a loss. And events very soon after proved that they had just cause for their regrets; for Italy being deprived of Lorenzo's counsels, no means could be found to satisfy or check the ambition of Lodovico Sforza, governor of the Duke of Milan. From this, soon after Lorenzo's death, there began to spring up those evil seeds of trouble, which ruined and continue to cause the ruin of Italy, as there was no one capable of destroying them.

Of how many kinds are republics and of what sort was the Roman republic*

There is no doubt that a mixed government, made up of the three powers, prince, optimates [patricians] and people, is better and more stable than government of one of these types alone. Particularly when it is mixed in such a way that of each kind the good qualities are taken, and the bad omitted. This is the important point to be noted where those setting up a government may go wrong. To discuss this in detail, I will say that the advantage of princely rule is that affairs are governed much better, in a more orderly manner, and with greater speed, secrecy and determination, when they depend on the will of one man alone, than when a number of people are involved. Its disadvantage is that when power falls into the hands of an evil man with the unfettered ability to do harm, all that authority he holds is used for evil. Likewise if he is not wicked, but lacks ability, infinite disasters arise out of his incapacity. And even if the king were chosen by election, not by inheritance, there is no absolute bar to such dangers, for the electors may easily be deceived, supposing a candidate to be good and prudent when he is nothing of the sort. And the extent of his power and freedom often changes the character of a man thus chosen, and especially if he has children it is hard for him not to desire their succession. Once he is king with absolute power, it is nearly impossible to prevent that happening, even though it may be forbidden by the constitution

* *Francesco Guicciardini: Selected Writings*, ed. C. Grayson, trans. M. Grayson, Oxford University Press 1965. 'Considerations on the *Discourses*'.

of the kingdom, yet he can only bring it about by arts and means which are far from praiseworthy.

Wishing therefore to set up a government sharing as much as possible the advantages of royal government, and lacking its bad points, it is not possible to enjoy all the benefits and avoid entirely its evils, and one must be satisfied with something less of the good, lest too many of the evils creep in. Hence the king must be elected for life but with limited authority, by arranging that he cannot decide anything on his own, or at any rate only those things of minor importance. In this manner one would have the advantage of one pair of eyes constantly watching public affairs, one head to whom they are referred, one procurator to propose, further and remember them. One would have the benefit of one man's decision and execution, but as this must involve the danger of giving him power to turn the state into a tyranny it is a lesser evil to enjoy fewer advantages with safety, than more involving such grave danger. Therefore let the king, that is, the leader standing in that position, have his authority limited in such a manner that he may not alone decide matters of importance; and let him be by election not by inheritance. Under these circumstances it is better that his term should be for life, rather than a limited one, yet if for a limited term, better long than short. In this the Venetians have done better than the Romans and Spartans, for the Spartan kings were always of the same family, and by succession, and the kings of Rome, though they had the senate and some vestiges of a republic, yet enjoyed such authority that it was easy for them to turn the kingdom into a tyranny, the beginnings of which were seen in Servius Tullius, and then openly in Tarquinius Superbus. And if you like to call the authority of the consuls royal, it was not perpetual but annual, whereas the Venetian prince is perpetual, elected, and enjoys strictly limited powers.

In government by the optimates there is this advantage, that being many they can less easily set up a tyranny than one man could. As they are the best qualified men in the city they rule it with more intelligence and prudence than a multitude might. And being publicly honoured they have less reason to intrigue, which they might easily do if discontented. The trouble is that as their authority is great they favour those measures useful to themselves and oppressive to the rest of the population, and as there are no bounds to men's ambition to increase their estate, they come into conflict with others like themselves, and commit acts of sedition. From this ensues the city's ruin, either through tyranny or by some other means; and if they are optimates by birth and not by election, from prudent and good men at first, affairs soon fall into the hands of imprudent and wicked ones.

In order to extract from this kind of government what is best and avoid what is worst, the optimates must not be drawn always from the same lines and families, but from the whole body of the city, from all who according to the law are qualified to take part in the magistrature, and a senate must be elected to deal with difficult matters, containing the flower of the prudent noble and rich men of the city. It should be perpetual, or have at least a very long term of office. The members should be very numerous so as to be more easily accepted by the others who will be able to hope that they or their house may succeed when vacancies occur. And also with a large number there is hope that all those who deserve to may enter. Even if some get in who are not suitable that is better than keeping out anyone who is well qualified. They should not hold absolute power over all public affairs, so as not to usurp too much authority, particularly in the matter of creating public officials, especially those with powers of punishment, either capital or for lighter offences, or those concerned with finances. They should not be permitted to make laws without the people's agreement so that they are able neither to change the form of the government nor to use the organisation of the city to the benefit of the powerful and oppression of the weak.

Their function must be to discuss and decide those matters where human prudence is most needed, that is, wars, peace, negotiations with princes, and all matters essential for the preservation and expansion of the state. The Spartans had optimates of this kind, drawn not from a special class of men but from the whole body of the city; the Romans had them, but differently, for with them the patricians were from the first the optimates and the rest formed the plebs, which was the origin of all their seditious movements.

One good thing about government by the people is that while it lasts there can be no tyranny. Laws are more powerful than men, and the proper end of all decisions is the safeguarding of universal well-being. The disadvantage is that the people, on account of their ignorance, are not capable of deciding matters of great importance, and so any republic which leaves the people to decide its affairs soon falls into decay. It is unstable and always looking for change, and yet easily deceived and misled by ambitious men and traitors. They are fond of persecuting well qualified citizens, for they need novelty and disturbances. To avoid these consequences one should not give the people power in any important matters, all except those which, were they in any other hands, would endanger freedom, such as the election of magistrates, the creation of laws. These should not come to the people until they have been well digested and approved by the supreme magistrates and the senate. However, the measures they put forward must not come into force until they are approved by the people. There should not be a free debate, for that is the principal instrument of sedition, but in the people's council only those who are invited by the magistrates to speak should do so, and only on the subject entrusted to them. By organising the state after this pattern you will obtain the balance described in the *Discourse*.